MW01141008

Hummingbirds & Hard Hats

The *Circle of Love* Story of Ingrid Reeves

Hummingbirds & Hard Hats

The *Circle of Love* Story of Ingrid Reeves
By Susan D. Brandenburg

Book and book cover design by Andie Jackson
Economy Printing of Jacksonville, Florida
www.EconomyPrinting.net

Final Editing by M.F.A. Shipp

ISBN: 978-09833848-0-9

This book was published in the U.S.A. by Susan the Scribe, Inc.
www.susanthescribe.vpweb.com

Table of Contents

Foreword

Colette Baron-Reid

The moment I set eyes on Ingrid I knew she was special. There was a palpable energy around her that pulsed with life and I could literally see a light surround her in a soft glow. Over the course of four years, Ingrid would attend all the events I was speaking at, and I watched her transformation as it unfolded. I've had the privilege to spend some time with her, get to know her journey and encourage her to tell her story to the world.

Her life is a testament to the survival of faith in spite of difficult beginnings, and a deep and true connection to the Great Mystery which Ingrid was born to unravel and reveal. The word "healer" describes Ingrid at her core for she is selfless in her giving and has an uncanny "knowing" of the life force that sings through all creatures, great and small. I won't spoil it for you by revealing the details (which you will read and hopefully savor through these pages).

I admire her greatly and know that anyone who reads this book will be deeply touched by its integrity, honesty and refreshing optimism and hope.

Colette Baron-Reid
#1 Bestselling author of *The Map, Finding the Magic and Meaning in the Story of Your Life*

Introduction

Ingrid Yvette Reeves

When we are born, we come into this world so innocent, all cultures and colors lying side by side in the hospital nursery. Then we are taken home by our parents.

Our infant hearts that are so ready to love and be loved, can sometimes be broken. So it was in my childhood. My mother forced me to work like a slave from the time I was five years old. She scornfully called me her "little gift." Because I was different, she hated me.

At age eight, upon learning that my mother had tried to sell me again, I attempted suicide, climbing to the top of a tall tree and throwing myself thirty feet to the ground. My arm was broken as a result of thc fall, but my broken heart miraculously began to heal that day.

As I grew older, even as the horrible abuse grew, my resolve to survive and thrive grew, too. I knew I was beautiful in God's view and I saw my beauty reflected in my mother's angry eyes. I saw the glory of the elements in every living creature and intuitively understood the delicate balance

between love and hate. The light of joy and the energy of purpose flowed inside me.

I smiled as I worked – and worked – and worked.

Later, as a wife, mother and business owner, I smiled as I worked – and worked – and worked.

I thrived on hard work. It was my lot in life.

When I wore my first pink hard hat, I was the only woman working on a tough, dirty, dangerous job that required hard hats and safety gear at all times. As the lady in the pink hard hat, I lived a life of extremes in the power plants where I worked for more than three decades with my husband, Richard – extreme temperatures, extreme pressures, extreme danger and extreme pride in a job well-done.

Today, my pink hard hat symbolizes another type of extreme. It is the extreme satisfaction of having worked hard and lived well. It is the extreme thrill of finding the path to happiness, health, wisdom and wealth. It is the extreme gratitude I feel for every moment of life. It is the extreme amazement within my soul that I have finally recognized my muse – the tiny hummingbirds that have always been there – sparkling in iridescent beauty, dancing in my heart, and populating my serene mountain home. I invite you to put on your pink hard hat and follow me as we climb my magical mountain of discovery, taste the sweet nectar of knowledge, soar to the heights of awareness, and join our hands and hearts in the Circle of Love.

Prologue

The hummingbird flew frantically in search of the sky, its tiny wings whirring as it repeatedly slammed into the hard surface of the thirty foot ceiling instead. Helplessly, Ingrid watched the tiny bird, her attention divided between the lecturer in the glass-enclosed room and the life and death struggle ensuing above.

"We were in a gorgeous lecture room on the fifth floor of the Blue Spirit Resort in Costa Rica," recalls Ingrid. Surrounded by lush tropical forest on all sides, the glassed-in room had a magical indoor-outdoor eye-tricking atmosphere that most assuredly had lured the little hummingbird to its horrid dilemma.

For nearly two hours, the beautiful bird beat its wings against the ceiling, and then, it gave up the battle and fell thirty feet to the floor. Running to the limp, lifeless little body, Ingrid crouched down and gently cupped her hands around the hummingbird. As she talked softly, urging it to live, live, live … she breathed warm, life-giving energy into her cupped hands. Within seconds, the lecturer, Colette Baron-Reid, was down on the floor next to Ingrid, talking, talking to the bird. "We love you, we love you … we're giving you energy … all

you need is to get your energy back!" Both of them saw the slight fluttering movement of the hummingbird. The breath caught in their throats as Colette pushed the tiny bird up closer into Ingrid's hands.

"It lay there, very still in my cupped hands, and I could feel its warmth and life flowing through it," recalls Ingrid. "I walked out to the glass slider that was open and held my hands far out, felt its wings flutter and then it flew away!"

A cheer went up from those in the lecture room who had witnessed the dramatic rescue.

"The cheering surprised me," said Ingrid. "I had forgotten anyone else was there. I was the hummingbird."

Indeed, Ingrid suddenly knew that she and the hummingbird were one. At age eight, Ingrid, like the hummingbird, was beaten down by forces beyond her control. Like the hummingbird, she finally gave up and fell, exhausted, from a height of thirty feet. And, like the hummingbird, despite hurts and challenges, she has received new energy to spread her wings and share her beautiful spirit with the world.

Chapter 1

Outcast

Ingrid climbed. Her face washed in tears, her small fingers digging furiously into the furrowed bark of the huge elm tree in her backyard, the little girl desperately pulled herself skyward. Crawling to the narrow end of a sturdy limb about thirty feet in the air, the child perched precariously. Scraped knees and dirty shoes dangling, she stared at the red tricycle on the back porch. It looked like a toy from up here. She squinted into shafts of sunlight slicing through the branches, peering at the distant ground below. A humming-bird darted by, its tiny wings whirring, its high-pitched bell-like chirp ringing in the silence. Then it was gone. All was quiet. She was alone. Eight-year-old Ingrid sighed, squared her thin shoulders, closed her eyes, leaned forward, reached for the sky, launched herself as if to fly, and fell to her death.

"I really wanted to die that day. My mother had tried to sell me again," recalls Ingrid Reeves, shuddering at the

memory of that dark time so many decades ago.

"I climbed that tree, determined to die, but I broke my left arm instead. Then I got really scared. What if Mums found out?"

For two weeks following her failed suicide attempt, the sad little shadow of a girl was able to hide her throbbing, swollen arm from her mother, her siblings and her teachers. Sure enough, upon discovering the broken bone, her mother, "Mums," screamed with anger – not because her daughter had hidden her injury, but because of the money a doctor visit would cost.

Money was short for Ingrid's family in 1956 – but never as short as her mother's temper. Fair-skinned, with blonde highlights glinting in her light brown hair and eager intelligence sparkling in her pretty brown eyes, eight-year-old Ingrid bore the brunt of her mother's anger daily. No matter what the child did, it seemed there was an impenetrable wall of ice around the heart of Josephine Olivier Marcus when it came to her youngest daughter. Ingrid was different and Josephine hated her for it.

The mother of six children by four fathers, Josephine Marcus was a tiny, dark, fiery woman at 4'9" tall. She was a native of Port of Spain, Trinidad – an exotic beauty with an insatiable appetite for alcohol, tobacco and men.

All of Josephine's children, with the exception of fair Ingrid, favored their mother's dusky islander appearance. The oldest daughter, Davis, nicknamed "Dee," had a voluptuous Italian look – dark, shining eyes and long straight hair; while Enid, eleven months younger than Davis, was the mirror image of her mother – a striking, nappy-haired island beauty.

Frank, a coffee-colored boy who grew up to look almost exactly like Barack Obama, was a year older than Ingrid. Walter, Jr., born when Ingrid was five years old, was the color of a bright copper penny – a boy whose multi-ethnic beauty was astounding - and Ury, the youngest boy, though of Puerto Rican descent, looked like an Arab from the Middle East.

Ingrid Yvette Marcus was born in Port of Spain, Trinidad on January 24, 1947, and taken as an infant by her father, Walter Marcus, to New York City.

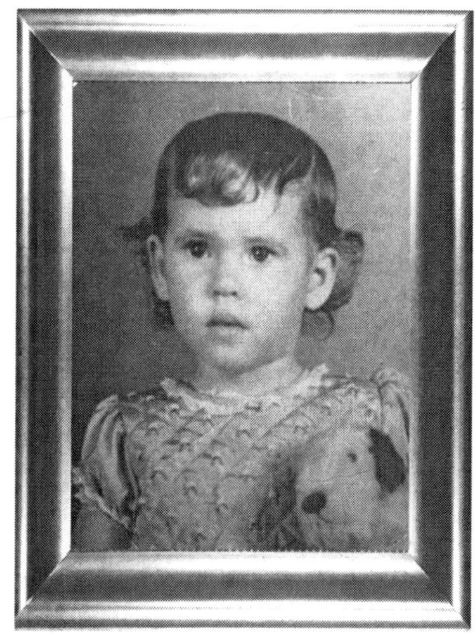

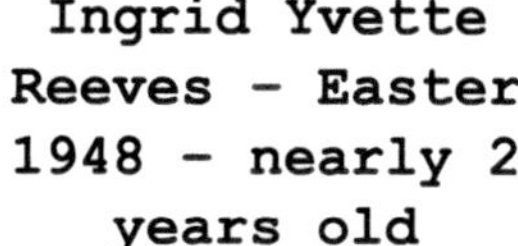

Ingrid Yvette Reeves - Easter 1948 - nearly 2 years old

For the first five years of her life, Ingrid lived alone with her father in an apartment at 57 Henry Street. Walter Marcus was a German Jew, born in Hamburg, whose parents were killed by the Nazis at Dachau in World War II. Walter was a Chief Steward in the Merchant Marines.

“Dad never talked much, and he wasn’t one to show much emotion. He was very quiet and spoke more German than English. My dad had the most beautiful blue eyes. I adored him, but I saw him only rarely because he was out to sea most of the time," recalls Ingrid. "When he was gone, there were caretakers for me in our New York apartment, but it was a strange, solitary life. Caretakers aren't paid to give you hugs and kisses."

When her father was in port, Ingrid remembers some astounding moments that later led her to believe he may have been a German spy for the U.S. government following World War II.

For instance, there was the time he took her to the U.N. Building in New York City and sat her down with a coloring book in the back of a large round room with many seats. The little girl colored happily while her father talked to a big gathering of people across the room.

Another time, he took her to the Empire State Building, where he briefly met with one of his bosses, the Greek millionaire Ari Onassis.

Still another odd encounter was the day that Walter took Ingrid to the Waldorf Astoria Hotel, where he had a breakfast meeting with Governor Rockefeller. Ingrid recalls that Governor Rockefeller gave her a dollar to go get some ice cream because they wanted to talk privately. "I bought a piece of apple pie with the dollar and they put what I thought was a scoop of ice cream on it, but it was cheese! Ugh!"

In later life, a couple of Walter's prize possessions were a photograph of himself with Harry Truman, and a plaque from President Dwight D. Eisenhower that credited him for preparing the best meals for the men on board ship for the least amount of money.

Josephine Marcus

Walter and Josephine Marcus

Walter's complete custody of his beautiful child for the first five years of her life was an indication of his protective love for her, but eventually, his love for her mother, Josephine, prevailed.

A lonely little girl who had no playmates, Ingrid was thrilled on the day that her father announced he was taking her to the airport to meet her mother and her siblings. All of a sudden, she had a real family!

"Mums" or "Mummie" arrived in New York with her children, Davis, Enid and Frank (Walter, Jr. and Ury were yet unborn). Although each of his wife's children was the product of a different father, Walter Marcus happily took them all into his heart and his home, giving them his name and claiming them as his own.

"Mums smiled and called me her little 'gift,' but she didn't treat me like a gift," says Ingrid. "Her smile didn't reach all the way to her eyes, and I saw that right away." From that first strange meeting at the airport until Josephine Marcus's death many years later, fear and anger dominated the relationship between Ingrid and her mother.

"Mums treated me differently. She was abusive to all of her children, but there was a certain level of horror that she saved just for me. I tried to fit in with my new family, but I looked like the milkman's child."

Indeed, nearly thirty years after the death of the man she knew as her father, Ingrid learned the truth. She was the daughter of a Nordic Irish seaman who enjoyed a drunken one-night-stand with her mother before sailing out of Port of Spain and out of her life forever.

"I'll always consider Walter Marcus my real, if not biological, dad. He loved me and I loved him. I loved my mother too, as much as I feared her."

Vignettes from Ingrid's childhood form a painful litany of turbulent times and troubled people:

- *"Dad went off to sea after the family got settled in our apartment and, pretty soon, Mums started having men visitors. She would invite them in and send us kids to bed. We'd hear them laughing and talking until late at night, but they'd be gone in the morning. Then she'd sleep half the day. She was an alcoholic and was usually hung over, but I didn't know anything about alcohol then. She'd say she was sick and I'd get cold washcloths for her head and try to take care of her."*
- *"We were raised Catholic. We went to mass and catechism, but Mums never darkened the door of a church.*
- *There was a giant crucifix hanging over her bed in the apartment in New York and I remember that when I passed her door, I ran! That bloody man on the cross scared the living daylights out of me!"*
- *"One day, a man came over with this little girl about my age and my mother told me I was to go to his house and play with his little girl. I was thrilled. He took me to his apartment, but then he put the little girl in one bedroom and took me to another bedroom. He closed the door and gave me this doll. It was a cloth doll – kind of a Raggedy Ann thing – and he showed me how to take the skirt and flip it – one side she'd be smiling – the other side, she'd be frowning. Then he went into the bathroom. Something inside told me to get out of there – fast! I jumped up and ran out and ran all the way home for blocks and blocks. I was only five years old, but somehow I knew my mother had taken money for me from that man. That was the first time she tried to sell me. I never told anyone and I never*

saw him again. After that, I was deathly afraid of my mother."

- *"I found out much later that I had every reason to be afraid of my mother. An intuitive told me, and my sister Enid confirmed it, that my mother was raped repeatedly by her eight brothers and her father. She had raging hatred inside her. She would have slit a man's throat in a minute."*
- *"Mums beat my sisters and brothers viciously with belts when she got angry, but she didn't beat me. I would fade off into a corner and sit there shaking. She would just look at me in disgust and walk away."*
- *"In 1992, after years of abusing alcohol and smoking cigarettes, Mums died of cancer in Hawaii. She died screaming. Before she died, she gave me that same old scornful look and said, 'You're still afraid of me, aren't you?'"*
- *"Once, when we were still in New York, Dad came into port and landed in the hospital with a nervous breakdown. Looking back, I suspect that's when he found out she tried to sell me. She must have told him then that I wasn't his child. I'll never know that for sure."*

In 1953, soon after the birth of Walter Raymond Marcus, Jr. (the only one of his children actually fathered by Walter Marcus), the family moved to the little seaside village of Patchogue, Long Island. There, they purchased a large 100-year-old home on a tree-lined street about two blocks from the Atlantic Ocean.

It was a strange life in Patchogue. Walter was out to sea most of the time and Josephine struggled to make ends meet by first opening a nightly janitorial service, then a construction company and, later, a restaurant. In each of these endeavors, she enlisted the help of her daughters, Enid and Ingrid.

- *"I was about six years old when Mums put me to work in the cleaning service. Enid was eleven. Dee had a heart murmur, so she never had to work. She stayed home with our brothers while we pushed those big waxing machines, scrubbed floors and washed the bathrooms at places like the A&P and Metropolitan Insurance Company every night, all night long. We finished up just in time to get to school."*
- *"My teachers thought I was mute. They said, 'What's wrong with this child?' I sat there like a zombie, so tired and so afraid to speak. Mums had warned us, 'Hide if the police come around. Don't tell anybody what we're doing. Don't say a word!' I knew better than to say a word!"*

Ingrid has never forgotten the pain of those long nights and the long school days that followed. In her poem, *Oh Lord, I'm Just a Child*, Ingrid describes being aroused by her mother at 2 a.m., to go clean and scrub offices. She remembers opening the doors to a huge conference room that suddenly turned, in her mind's eye, into a magnificent ballroom.

> *"Mirrored sphere, suspended in air, it whirls, twirls, luminous color beaming. A handsome prince, may I have this dance. Violins, harpsichords, mandolins,*

flutes . . Door flies open, my mop drops with a clatter,
CHILD! What is the matter, a voice screams with scorn
– scrub, clean. There's an abundance more.
Oh Lord, I'm just a child."

Ironically, the hard work forced upon her as a very young child has benefitted Ingrid all of her life. She learned to escape into her imagination. She learned that she had a reserve of strength and ability far beyond her physical age and size. When she reached the edge of her endurance and felt herself falling into the deep abyss of hopelessness, young Ingrid learned to gird herself with the courage and determination it took to finish the job. Today, she retains that amazing tenacity. It is an inadvertent gift from her mother. It is a lasting legacy left to Josephine's little "gift."

- *"The day I climbed the elm tree in our backyard was one of the worst days of my life. Two bad things caused me to want to die that day:*

    First, my mother tried to sell me again. I heard her talking to Mrs. Hayman, our Jewish neighbor next door, and offering to sell me to her for $10,000. Mrs. Hayman had two baby boys that I loved. Mrs. Hayman bought the dress for my first holy communion. But Mrs. Hayman couldn't believe my mother was trying to sell me to her. Mothers don't do that.

    The other thing that happened that day was even worse – I experienced my first taste of real prejudice and I couldn't bear it. My new

friends in the neighborhood had just told me they weren't allowed to play with me anymore because their parents had found out my family was 'colored.' That was when I climbed the tree."

- *"My mother bought new things for my brothers and sisters, but she never bought anything for me. I wore hand-me-downs and stuffed my shoes with cardboard. If Mrs. Hayman hadn't bought me the communion dress, I wouldn't have felt so pretty that day. Dad bought the flowers. He didn't know about the way Mums treated me because he usually wasn't there. I was the only one of her children she ever tried to sell.*

- *Even my violin was a gift from someone else. There was a teacher at school who thought I had musical talent. He gave me a violin and free violin lessons. I had to walk two miles to his house, across a high corn field, but it was worth it. I loved playing the violin and I played for the orchestra in New York several times. New York was a wonderful place for the arts, but when I got to California, there was no orchestra and I didn't play my violin anymore."*

- *"We didn't celebrate holidays or birthdays when I was growing up. We never had Christmas trees or presents, either. Sometimes we'd go to the woods and get our own tree, decorate it with paper and popcorn and berries – collect enough soda bottles to buy her a present. She'd always say the same thing: 'I don't want a present. I just want you kids to be good.' We were good."*

- *"It took something as serious as a hemorrhage or worse for Mums to justify spending money on a doctor. None of us ever wanted to admit we needed medical attention because she would get so angry. I was so afraid to tell her when I felt sick, that I would take a spoon full of sugar, put it in water, and hope for a cure."*

- *"We once had a fire in that big old house. I was about ten years old and I had escaped to my favorite place in the house – the attic. That's where I practiced playing my violin to the howling accompaniment of my poor dog, Demash. The others were on the second floor sleeping. The fire started behind the couch in the living room – one of the electrical sockets sparked – and Demash ran downstairs barking and getting everybody up. Mums threw a blanket under running water in the bathtub and ran us all out of the house under that blanket.*

- *"The fire gutted the whole house and we rebuilt it from the sheetrock on up, knocking down the burnt stuff and carrying it out in buckets. Mums had a construction business by then, and she was in charge of rebuilding and restoring the house. I remember that she was putting upthe last piece of wall paper when she began hemorrhaging and we called the ambulance. She was about to give birth to Ury, but she had to finish the house first."*

- *"When Mums started the construction company, running bulldozers and other heavy equipment and doing reconstruction, Enid and I helped with that, too. We were also involved in gathering materials like door knobs and hardwood flooring and crystal from homes that were about to be demolished. I remember one day when I was pulling nails out of boards and a nail went clear through my foot. Mums poured kerosene and salt on it. The pain was incredible, but the wound healed."*

- *"Dad would come into port in Florida at Cape Canaveral or wherever, and Mums would go to him and take me with her. A few times, we stayed in a trailer in Jacksonville when he was in port. He always told her, 'Don't you come see me without Ingrid.' I was his favorite child, even though he loved the others, too."*

- *"As chief steward on ocean liners, Dad was in charge of all the food – he was an awesome cook. When he came home to Long Island, he would cook spaghetti from scratch – cooking the sauce for days. I remember it had eggshells floating in the stock, and then he'd strain it with a cheese cloth. He made the best bread in the world. When asked how he made such delicious bread, he said that when they were way out to sea, he used salt water and that was his secret ingredient."*
- *"We loved it when Dad came home. It was the only time we knew, for sure, we'd have enough to eat, and it was the only time the neighborhood kids would play with us. Dad was very white. When he was home, the neighborhood kids played baseball with us, but when he left, they stayed away."*
- *"Dad must have given Mums some money, but we never saw any of it. Sometimes, she'd stay away for a couple of days and leave us completely without food, especially after she opened the restaurant in Central Islip, Long Island. It was called Felicia's Diner – Felicia is Enid's middle name. Mums was a good cook and when Dad was in port, he cooked at the restaurant, too. They made wonderful doughnuts and lemon meringue pies.*
- *"It was either feast or famine for us. The restaurant was quite a distance away and when Mums stayed overnight there, we had to fend for ourselves. Sometimes there were only a few potatoes and we'd make potato soup and live*

on that until she came home. Enid was sixteen by then and she taught me how to make the 'Bake,' with just flour and water and salt and baking soda – you could mix it together and roll it out and fry it. The bake and potato soup was all we had to eat when Mums stayed at the restaurant."

- *"I remember one time sitting at the Atlantic Ocean just down the road from our house and looking at a huge pile of white sand on the beach. The longer I stared, the more it looked like a pile of coconut. It was a coconut mirage for a hungry girl who loved coconut."*

- *"Once, when I traveled to a poor country with Dad, I saw a little girl and boy standing by a curb. As our car passed by, some people threw a banana peel at them and the little girl picked it up and yelled, 'Thank you!' She began gnawing on the banana peel, but then the little boy grabbed it away and she cried. I cried, too. I knew what it was to be hungry."*

- *"Speaking of bananas, there was a pretty memory I had when I was about five years old: My sisters, Enid and Dee, were babies lying together in one crib, both of them drinking from a banana-shaped bottle that had nipples on either end. The sun was shining in on them from a window behind the crib. There were purple morning glories in the window and hummingbirds flitting around. It was a beautiful scene, with the two babies in the white wrought-iron crib framed by that window full of flowers and birds. Even at five years old, I must have been intuitive because I remember that scene so vividly and yet, I could not have seen it in reality because Enid and Dee were older than I was and they were in Trinidad when they were babies – before I was born. I know it wasn't a dream because I asked Enid about that banana bottle with two nipples, and the white crib and the window and she was stunned when I described the scene, because it was just as she remembered – in fact, she said that Dee would suck real hard on her end and get all the milk and she would lay there and cry, looking out through her tears at the morning glories and hummingbirds."*

- *"Enid knew what it was like to be hungry, and so did I. Enid was my closest sibling. She tried to protect me from Mums, but we were all her victims. Mums always tried to get us to sleep with her. The other kids did, but I didn't. She couldn't make me. When I was very young, I had to share a bed with Dee, but I scooted to the very edge to keep away from her. Like Enid, I found out that Dee could be very selfish and mean-spirited. One night, I threw my arm over in my sleep and hit her by mistake. She kicked me so hard in the back that I've had back problems all my life. After that, I slept alone – even if I had to sleep on the floor."*

- *"My sister, Enid, looked and acted more like Mums the older she got. By the time Enid was sixteen, Mums had already spent a lot of her money on abortions for her. I remember that I had two little gold bracelets from Dad, but Mums took them to pay for one of Enid's abortions."*

- *"One of the happiest days of my life was when Dad brought me home a little Madame Alexander doll when I was four or five years old. She had brown hair and blue eyes and a polka dot dress and white high heeled shoes, which I promptly lost. I put glue on her feet and sprinkles where her shoes had been. I played with her until she was almost threadbare. Dad brought me other porcelain dolls over the years, but that's the one I remember the best."*

- *"Not long after Mums opened the restaurant, a man borrowed her Pontiac station wagon to drive Dee and Enid to a high school dance. They got into a horrible accident and both girls were badly injured. Enid broke her pelvic bone and was in a body cast for nearly a year. Mums got sued by the other parties in the accident and she lost everything – our home, our restaurant – everything. I remember we had to walk to the hospital to see Enid and Dee.*
- *"I was paranoid about germs after Enid and Dee spent that long time in the hospital in New York. Mums kept telling us not to drink out of the fountains or touch anything because of the germs. If anybody touched my fork or my food, I pushed it away. Germs were horrible. I didn't want those germs. Mums had me scared to death."*
- *"For about four months before we moved to California, we moved from Patchogue to Brooklyn and lived in a small apartment at 424 Ashford Street. That was when a man named Phil Ginsberg came into the picture. He was going with Enid and he sat around hearing my mother say,' Ingrid do this! Ingrid do that! Ingrid do this! Ingrid do that!' Until he started joking around, calling me 'Cinderella.' "Cinderella, do this! Cinderella, do that!"*
- *"Finally, Mums bought a little white Nash Rambler, piled*

the whole family into it, and we drove cross-country to Bloomington, California."

- *"There were TEN of us in that little Nash Rambler – Mums, Dad, Frank, Walter, Jr., Ury, Dee, Enid and her new husband, Phil Ginsberg, me, and . . . oh yes, Enid's unborn son, Kennith (but that's for another story!).*

It was 1961 … a tough time for a mixed-race family to be traveling across the country in an old Nash Rambler or any other form of transportation. It was a tough time for Ingrid, too, as she would be the one called upon to go inside for food. Colored people weren't allowed in many restaurants back then. There were separate restrooms and water fountains, and "Whites Only" signs were posted everywhere.

Ingrid was the only child in the car who could pass the barriers set up by the Jim Crow society of the 60s. In some states, her dad would have been arrested for being married to her mother.

"They were my family and I was not ashamed of them. It hurt to see my brothers and sisters and my mother having to go around back. Most of the time, my mother would sit in the car. I knew then that I was not the only outcast in my family. We all were."

Outcasts are not always the ugly ones or the bad ones. Ingrid was an outcast from the moment she was born. Knowing the pain of rejection and scorn, both from society and from her own family, her silent resolve to heal rather than hurt has helped her navigate troubled waters as she journeyed through the rapids and oceans, mountains and valleys of life.

"When you're in the womb," Ingrid says, "the first

organ that is formed is the heart. The second is the brain. We must think first with our heart and then with our brain, and then again, with our heart. A circle of compassion – heart to brain to heart – that is what has completed me as a person. That is the hope I can offer to others who are outcasts like I was."

Ingrid's poems reflect her loving, lyrical, non-judgmental philosophy. An excerpt from one of her poems reads as follows:

> *"Do not judge a person by physical appearance or color. Listen to their words. Watch their actions. For then, you will hear the beat of their heart and know the notes to the music."*

Looking back at her troubled early childhood, Ingrid points to the long, tearful climb of a small eight-year old girl up to the top branches of a tall elm tree. It was an epiphany and an omen.

"I'm shocked that I was desperate enough, at that young age, to want to end my life," she marvels. "No child should have to bear the burden of abuse and prejudice. And yet, as we made our way to California and I walked into restaurant after restaurant that my family could not enter, I knew that I would spend the rest of my life climbing one elm tree or another in my quest to keep other outcasts from giving up and taking a fall."

Advice From a Hummingbird™
Dear friend,
Sip the sweet moments
Let your true colors glow
Be a nectar-collector
Dive into possibilities
Take yourself lightly
Express the joy of Your True Nature
Blossom in your own little sphere
Zoom in when you are needed
Good things come in small packages
Don't get your feathers ruffled over little things
Some days are just a humdinger
Take delight in being noticed
Change directions easily
Let your dreams take flight
Just wing it
Keep your visits short and sweet!
Ilan Shamir

Chapter 2

Cinderella Cheerleader

We are the Bruins!
The Mighty Mighty Bruins!
We are the Bruins!
The Mighty Mighty Bruins!

When Ingrid tried out for cheerleading at the brand new Bloomington High School in 10th grade, it was a huge leap for that former "mute" first-grader.

"It was a fresh start. No one knew me or my family. I really thought I wanted to be a cheerleader because I wanted to be as close to the action on the field as I could possibly get, but looking back, I realize I also wanted to feel close to my classmates because I didn't feel that close to my family at home."

Ingrid was in math class when they announced the names of the new Bloomington Bruins Cheerleading Squad over the school PA system.

"When my name was announced, I shouted 'YES!' and shocked everybody in class," recalls Ingrid, grinning at the memory. "Most of them, including my math teacher, Mr. Johnson, had never heard me say a word before that day."

The Marcus family's cross-country sojourn had culminated in the purchase of a ten acre plot of land with a little Sears Roebuck house sitting on it.

"We were on Willow Street, and the house was a lot like the Sears Roebuck kit house that Richard Nixon's father built in Yorba Linda, California. It was a small house, but somehow we all fit in there just fine."

Sears Roebuck kit homes were fairly common throughout the United States during the 50's and 60's, despite the fact that Sears discontinued their catalogue sales of the homes in 1940. According to author Rosemary Thornton, the leading expert on the history of the fabricated homes offered by Sears, there were about 70,000 kit homes sold between 1908 and 1940, with more than 370 house design models available.

Sears Roebuck promised that “a man of average abilities could assemble a Sears kit home in about ninety days,” wrote Thornton. “No detail was overlooked, as both manual and blueprints instructed homeowners as to the correct spacing of the seven hundred and fifty pounds of nails.”

“We liked the Sears house. I slept on the porch, and we were thrilled because on either side of the acreage, there was a sweet potato patch and an orange grove,” recalls Ingrid. “The owners told us kids we were free to eat as many oranges and sweet potatoes as we wanted. We knew we’d never go hungry again!”

In addition to enjoying the sweet riches surrounding the acreage, Josephine was soon tilling a flourishing vegetable garden in the backyard and Ingrid was tending daily to the farm animals that came with the property (cows, chickens and pigs). Yes, although the little Sears house was overflowing with children, the heavy chores fell to only one of them – Ingrid. With Enid pregnant and married, and soon to move back to New York with her new husband, Ingrid’s life-long work partner was out of the picture. Josephine now turned her focus totally on Ingrid, forcing her, as always, to earn her place in the family through hard work.

Soon, Ingrid was back in the routine of cleaning homes and offices with her mother by night and going to school by day, except that there were now added responsibilities both at home and school.

“I would get up at 5 a.m. and feed the animals before I headed to school. Sometimes, I had only been in bed for an hour or two because we’d been out all night scrubbing floors and cleaning toilets.”

"I was really quiet in school, except when I was cheering – and then I let it all out! The rest of the time, I still was under Mums' command of silence when it came to talking about anything to do with our family. It was as if my family didn't exist when I went to school – not because I ignored them, but because Mums and the others were never there. Other cheerleaders and athletes had their families at games, but not me."

"Dad had a roll of money in his pocket with a rubber band around it when he came home. He must have been sending Mums money all along, but she always acted like she was poor. When I became a cheerleader, there was no money to buy a uniform. I had to work all summer at the school and at cleaning jobs to save money for the uniform, and then I could only afford a couple of pairs of the special gold socks we had to wear with our cheerleading uniforms. Our colors were blue and gold. At PE, though, we were only allowed to wear white socks. I couldn't afford both gold and white, so I always got demerits at PE and GAA (Girls Athletic Association) for wearing gold socks."

"Mums never talked to me about sex. I thought you got pregnant from a toilet seat, really! If I ran into a nasty toilet seat, I'd think, 'Oh dear, I hope I'm not pregnant.'"

"Enid gave me a sexy book called <u>Candy</u> before she left for New York because she said I didn't know anything! Mums was so mad when she saw that I was reading that book. She said it was trash. 'What are you reading that trash for?' she asked. 'Just read the Bible. It's all there in the Bible.' She was always quoting the Bible, even though she didn't go to church."

"I heard about date rape in high school, but I didn't date anyway – and then when a nice boy asked me out to a dance, I was really excited. I loved to dance better than anything! We had to walk through the park to get to the dance and he attacked me. I beat the crap out of him."

"I was 5 feet, 4 inches tall and I was strong. I had muscles like the guys. When my brother, Frank, and his friends lifted weights, I used to sneak in after they left and see if I could lift the same ones. I always could."

"I could beat the guys in arm wrestling and I had bulging muscles in the calves of my legs. I wasn't proud of my muscles because I wanted to look feminine and pretty – so I wore long sleeves when I could and didn't flex my arms or legs, but could I ever dance! Dancing was my favorite past-time – I liked it even more than surfing."

"Surf music was really in and I was a California girl, so I became a surfer girl beginning in 9th grade and surfed on a second-hand long board at Doheny Beach. I loved it and I was good at it, even though I only got to go a couple of times a month on weekends. If I helped him work on cars, my older brother Frank would take me to the beach in the van. He got a boat when he was about twenty-one and took me water skiing a few times, too."

"Sometimes I'd body surf with the dolphins in Huntington Beach. The water was very cold and I couldn't afford a wetsuit – but it was worth it."

"Enid got married and had Kennith when she was 18 – then

she and Phil Ginsberg moved to Flatbush, New York – a Jewish Orthodox area. Enid was a display artist in the windows of boutique stores. I learned later that she sent all kinds of beautiful clothes back to me in California, but I never saw any of them. My sister, Dee, and my mother were always beautifully dressed, but I never had any clothes except the ones I earned by working for them."

"Of all my siblings, Enid was the one who cared for me the most. She protected me. She and Frank fought like cats and dogs. She was like a mother figure to me. I remember one time she had pneumonia and the doctor came to the house. I heard him say, 'She's too far gone. She's going to die.' I was standing by the door and I began to wail, 'Enid! Please don't leave me! What am I going to do without you? Please don't die! What am I going to do without you?'"

"Thank God, Enid didn't die. Later, when she was better, she told me she had a near-death experience. She was going up this beautiful staircase and at the top of the staircase, a gorgeous angel waited with her arms open wide and her face shining with love – so much love! Enid was going to her and then she heard me screaming. She came back only because I needed her."

But Enid was married and gone by the time Ingrid began cheering in 10th grade at the new school, and so was a great deal of Ingrid's shyness. Although she remained mute about anything that was happening at home, Ingrid soon gained a reputation around school as the girl who was born with a smile on her face. Her smile was so constant that it was almost contagious, and apparently, it spoke too loudly to Mr. Rogers, the French teacher.

Ingrid remembers sitting in the French 2 class, smiling as she listened to Mr. Rogers drone on and on. "He looked over at me and scolded me for talking!" she recalls, still indignant. "I wasn't talking! I was just smiling. He made me cry. It hurt me deeply. I quit French and worked as an office monitor during that period from then on."

Still smiling a perpetual sunny smile, and still sensitive, Ingrid looks back on that incident as one of the rare sad moments she endured during her extremely happy high school career.

Another sad moment for Ingrid is a memory shared by nearly everyone in her "baby boomer" generation. That moment occurred on November 22, 1963, the day that President John Fitzgerald Kennedy was assassinated by gunman Lee Harvey Oswald in Dallas, Texas. That day, Ingrid remembers, her math teacher came out to lower the flag to half mast. "The President's been killed. No, no, no – that can't be true!" As the office monitor, Ingrid ran from classroom to classroom that day, delivering notes to the teachers as tears streamed down her face.

"We dedicated our high school annual to Jackie Kennedy," says Ingrid. "There was a picture in the yearbook of her at the funeral holding hands with Caroline and John. It was one of the saddest pictures I've ever seen."

The Class of '65 was Ingrid's class. It was also Bloomington High School's first graduating class.

"We started in 9th grade at another school and then in tenth, we all started together at Bloomington. Every year they

added another class below us until we graduated, so we were upper classmen all three years," remembers Ingrid. "It was an exciting time to be in high school. I was full of school spirit and I wanted our teams to WIN!"

Although she was known around school for her beautiful smile, Ingrid kept her distance from the other students, carefully avoiding the cliques. She gave everyone the same respect, spreading her cheerful energy around, but rarely becoming close to anyone. In addition to having to be close-mouthed about family, Ingrid had demands on her time that were beyond the imagination of most of her classmates.

Looking back on those high school days, Carol Wackerle O'Connell of Granite Bay, California, recalls that she and Ingrid were close enough in size that the two girls once swapped uniforms for an assembly that featured routines by both the Song Leaders and the Cheerleaders.

"I was a song leader when Ingrid was a cheerleader and we knew each other, but we didn't run around outside of school," recalls Carol. "Ingrid was closer in high school to my best friend, Carol Proud, but we've gotten to know one another much better in recent years at high school reunions."

What Carol O'Connor does remember about Ingrid is that "she was always friendly and smiling and seemed very happy." Strangely enough, now that nearly five decades have passed, Carol has discovered that she and Ingrid had much more in common back in high school than they ever imagined. A friendly, smiling song leader who danced and laughed and shook pompoms at school, Carol Wackerle, like Ingrid, dreaded going home.

"I, too, had an unhappy home life," recalls Carol.

"School was the only place where I could be free. It was the only place where I could be me."

While Bloomington High School was a blessed escape for Ingrid from another life filled with thankless hard work and the cold, constant scorn of her mother, for Carol, the school represented an opportunity for leadership. At home, Carol's parents made her every decision for her, giving her no credit for intelligence or discernment, but at the new school, she was a visible decision-maker.

"I was on the student council and we got to pick the school colors and the mascot!" Carol remembers proudly, still recalling the euphoria that came with making historic choices that would forever be a part of the high school experience for future generations.

"We chose the same colors as UCLA – Blue and Gold – and the Bruins were our mascot. We were the first. It was really exciting!" Carol also recalls that the class of '66 and the class of '65 were very close because they had been in 7th and 8th grade together and moved to the new school simultaneously (9th and 10th grades).

Having come to California just in time to be part of the transition from the old to the new school as a member of the Class of '65, Ingrid has forever felt a certain pride of ownership in Bloomington High School. She has never missed a reunion, and now that the 50th is approaching, the aging but energetic Class of '65 is growing close again.

"We're trying to start having annual picnics at the big park in Riverside where we used to go in high school," said Carol, noting that she just re-connected with Ingrid about six years ago. "We're all older now and not as willing to get up and dance," admits Carol, "but Ingrid still loves to dance and she gets us all out on the floor. Last time, she got us in a big circle and was showing us the dance moves. She is an amazing woman who still loves to dance and never seems to run out of energy!"

Energy and Ingrid are synonymous. For as far back as she can remember, it was a matter of necessity for her to pick herself up and keep going, no moping or stalling allowed!

"In my Junior year, I made a Class Double A Card, which meant I had straight A's! My gym teacher, who was also in charge of Girls Athletic Association, was Ms. Segovia, and she vowed nobody would get an A in PE. I was the only one who got one. I was teacher's pet. She used to call me 'Ingie!'"

"I worked all summer at the school, helping with the kindergarten class, and then babysat for the principal and his wife and cleaned their house. I also helped the Superintendent of Schools, Dr. Smith, after he came back from a trip to Russia. I typed all of his notes for him. He ended up being the curator at the museum in San Bernardino, California."

"Carol Proud was my one good friend in high school. She became my friend the last part of my senior year and we went to Valley Junior College together in San Bernardino. Her dad was the Agriculture Teacher in Fontana. She would ask her dad if she could go to a party and he'd always say no until she told him 'Ingrid is driving,' and then he'd say yes. I didn't drink in high school so I was always the designated driver."

Carol Proud Harvey enjoys reminiscing about those

days when she and Ingrid kicked off their shoes and did the surfer stomp at Dick Dale dances in San Bernardino. The Beach Boys were popular back then and the Righteous Brothers, the Jackson Five, Jan and Dean and Diana Ross … the music was groovy and life was good. Ingrid and her family fascinated young Carol Proud, who came from a very different background, indeed.

Carol Proud Harvey and Ingrid - Still great friends

"My home life was very structured and my parents were strict," recalls Carol Proud (now Harvey). "My dad was a teacher and Ingrid's dad was a merchant marine. Her mom was not like any of the other moms I knew. She was from Port of Spain, dark and secretive. She wasn't warm to us, Josephine. She had an all-knowing personality, kind of like a mystical person. She didn't seem interested in us at all."

Noting that Ingrid never talked about her childhood or

her family, Carol nevertheless observed certain things when she visited at the Marcus home.

"Their house was cluttered, with stuff piled high and sheets covering things," she recalls. "Ingrid's brother, Frank, was allowed to entertain his girlfriend, Candy, in the house. That would never have been allowed at my house. It was a different kind of life than I was used to."

For some reason that Carol still can't completely fathom, her very strict parents had total trust in Ingrid. As long as she was in Ingrid's company, Carol was allowed more freedom than she had ever had in her life.

"I was very open with my parents and they knew that Ingrid and I were good girls," recalls Carol. "But it was more than that … I don't know … maybe they were just enamored of her, too. Ingrid had a gift and she still does to this day. It is captured in her face. The way she just smiles and is open to people. Well, people respond to that. They want to be around her – they want to know her."

Describing Ingrid as "a rare beauty," Carol talks of her friend's "shiny, sparkly brown eyes, big dimples, big smile."

"Ingrid was very attractive and her scruples were so high," says Carol. "She knew intuitively how to stay away from trouble and my parents sensed that. Ingrid was the one person in my life who opened up my world for me. She said, 'Carol, just smile.' Her gift to me was that she gave me the inner confidence that I lacked before I knew her. That gift has remained with me forever. I'll always have the deepest, warmest spot in my heart for her."

Laughing about those days of driving to dances with Ingrid in the white Ford van, Carol remembers one occasion when a carload of boys was driving alongside and Ingrid turned the windshield wipers outward on the van and squirted the boys. "We had so much fun, just joking and laughing and dancing," she recalls.

"Ingrid was a boy trap," says Carol. "We were constantly being followed by groups of boys. Ingrid wasn't about that. She wasn't out to meet guys – she just wanted to dance and laugh and have a good time, but you couldn't walk anywhere with her without five or six guys following behind."

Speaking of guys, Carol remembers watching Ingrid's brother, Frank, work on cars. Frank bought a boat and took the girls to the Salton Sea to water ski.

Carol didn't think much, one way or the other, about the unusual variety of skin colors that ran through her friend's family. "Ingrid's family was so culturally different that I just found it fascinating," she says, recalling how she enjoyed the farm-like atmosphere on the acreage that surrounded the ranch house where Ingrid's family lived.

"Ingrid and I would climb in the white van and ride to the Safeway to pick up throw-away produce for pig-food," said Carol. "There were animals all over the place at her house and Ingrid always had chores to do."

"I drove my mother's old Econoline Ford van in my senior year. I had to go to the Safeway and the man in charge of the produce would pile up boxes of throwaway lettuce leaves for me. I would take the seats out of the van and take the boxes of vegetables back to the animals."

"A girl named Patricia, who came from a Catholic family with 22 children, wanted to be my friend because of my brother,

Frank. He always had a bunch of guys over working on cars. She was more interested in the guys than in me. She would spend the night and I'd ask her, 'Don't you have to call your parents and tell them where you are? She'd say no – they wouldn't even miss her – and I found out later that it was true. They ate in shifts, took baths in shifts – he worked at Kaiser Steel and he 'owed his soul to the company store.' It was a true Catholic family all right – he'd worn out and replaced a few wives by the time all those children were born!"

"Speaking of Catholic, by the time I was in 10th grade, I'd decided I didn't want to go to church anymore. I thought my Catholic classmates were hypocritical. They would do everything and then they'd go to confession and say a few prayers and all was forgiven. I thought it was utterly hypocritical. I wanted to know what confession was all about, but I had nothing bad to confess. I lied once just to get into the confessional. I said I stole my brother's pencil, but I didn't. I lied."

"I was so tired most of the time from working all night that my homework was half-done a lot of the time, but somehow I managed to keep my grades at A's and B's because I wanted to be part of the GAA and play all the sports. I played basketball, baseball, volleyball and track and I loved them all, even though I still had some severe back pain sometimes from when my sister Dee kicked me."

"None of the kids at school ever guessed that I was scrubbing floors to buy my cheerleading uniforms, but Mums and I were once caught scrubbing the floor at my English teacher's mother's house. She never said anything after that, but she

gave me better grades. She knew I had the ability – I just was too tired to study."

"My mother didn't go out in public – she was never seen at my school. She didn't even go to my graduation. She would still be gone sometimes for a couple nights at a time, but we didn't go hungry anymore in California because of the farm animals and the sweet potatoes and oranges."

"Mums had a beautiful body and Dad would bring her those Chinese silk dresses with the slit up the side. He loved the way they looked on her."

"One time, when I was a senior in high school, she acted almost normal for about two months. She joined the opera society at one of the colleges and sang as one of the cast. I was thrilled and I went to watch when they performed The Gypsy Baron. I remember there was a cast party afterwards and she was wearing a wig and while she was dancing, the wig flew off her head. Some man picked it up and put it back on her head and we all laughed. It was one of the rare laughs that I shared with my mother."

"I didn't talk with her or anybody else about her any more than I had to – I was afraid I'd say something wrong. I just felt so bad that people were so prejudiced against our family."

"I didn't get asked out much in high school. The boys would find out Frank Marcus, the guy who fixed up cars, was my brother, and that was it. All of the other cheerleaders were prejudiced and would say things in front of me, but they didn't know about my family. I was just very private. I listened and

smiled a lot, but I didn't talk."

"The strangest thing was that my mother was prejudiced against black people from Africa! She believed all the stereotypes – that they were lazy and immoral – it was really strange because my own sister, Dee, who looked like Sophia Loren, wouldn't let Mums or Enid in her beauty shop because they looked black with their nappy hair and dark skin."

"The few people I got close to in high school just assumed that they were not my real family. They thought that my dad was my dad, but I was from a previous marriage of his. Sometimes, I still think that might be the case, but one way or the other, it doesn't really matter now because he wasn't actually my dad either. It was all very confusing then ... still is."

"We moved from the Sears & Roebuck house on ten acres to a ranch house on twenty acres, but I still did all the chores. I remember that we had an old wringer washer and a cement sink at the Sears House. I always did all the clothes for all of us – I was in charge of the wash. I'd hang them out on the line before I went to school and make sure to feed the pigs and cows and chickens and rabbits, too."

"I had to get a paper signed and came home early from school. I opened the door and there was a man in Mums' bedroom. I piled pillows on the couch to make it look like somebody was visiting and sleeping on the couch in case someone saw him – so they wouldn't know he was sleeping in her bedroom."

"I laughed with Enid when that movie 'Slum Dog Millionaire' came out. Those people didn't have anything on us!"

"I led two separate lives – the one at home and the one at school. With so few close friends and so little time, not many people knew about my home life at all."

"The other cheerleaders were never really my friends – Sandy, Lita, Cindy and me ...there were only four of us, and the mascot – a girl named Judy Davis who dressed up like a Bruin. I hung with the bear. I'd do stuff with her to make everybody laugh."

"I have a trophy from cheerleading – from when we went to State. I was the only one on our squad who got a trophy. I was so excited! It was for being the most energetic cheerleader."

"We had GAA Letter Sweaters. Mine was white, with a blue and gold B for Bruins. It had pins and patches all over it from all of the sports. I loved being a cheerleader because it was close to the field. If I wasn't playing, I was cheering for the players. Looking back, I wanted to cheer, also, because it was a way of getting the acceptance from my school that I didn't get from home."

"I asked Dr. Smith, the superintendent of schools, if we could hold dances at the museum in Bloomington on the weekends. I must have been in 11th grade then. We held dances there until one night when some of the boys broke something and then those dances were over ... it was a museum, after all."

"Dick Dale had a band and did all the surfing music – we went to the Armory in Riverside and went to Roof Top Dances at Lake Arrowhead. Carol and I went to the Victorville Fair, too, and, after we sold hamburgers and hot dogs from her dad's trailer and made enough money, we'd go to the dance at the fair."

"We just laughed and had so much fun when Carol and I were together. Sometimes we'd get a group together and go marching down the street, pretending to be instruments. I started a lot of that kind of thing because I loved to make people laugh."

"In Senior English class, I wrote poems for everybody. We all had to turn in a poem, and everybody turned one in, but they were all written by me! I always loved writing poetry. I didn't keep any of my poems from high school, but I remember one about the earth looking like a palette of beautiful colors – with

all the seasons running together. I even cut out a cardboard palette and wrote the poem on it."

"My brother, Frank, was a great mechanic. He worked on everybody's car – they loved drag racing their cars and he could really fix them up. I used to help him so that he'd give me rides to the beach and to other places. I got to know all the parts of the cars pretty well. I didn't mind getting greasy. I was used to hard work."

"Frank was the only one that Mums would allow to use her sewing machine because, she said, he was the only one who could fix it if he broke it. The rest of us had to stay away from it. He could sew anything, and Mums was a wonderful seamstress. In fact, when she was doing a job, she worked hard and did well ...she was a very smart woman. It was just that she played hard, too."

"Dad retired from the Merchant Marines when I was in 11th grade. He just came home and mostly sat in front of the television set – loved watching the news or anything political, but if something about the Holocaust came on, he'd turn it right off. He lost his entire family in the Holocaust. He had the tattoo from the concentration camp on his arm – always wore long sleeved shirts to cover it up."

"Dad was a great cook. He helped with the cooking after he retired, too."

"I never did know what my dad's real connection was to the government. One thing happened when I was 18 that I'll never forget. I asked for my birth certificate because I wanted to get a job and found out that I wasn't a citizen of the United States

of America. Walter, my dad, said, 'Wait a minute, Ingrid. You're an alien. I've been filling out these green cards for you all these years.' I told him I was going to L.A. and become a citizen. He said, 'I'm going with you. You're illegitimate. I'm not married to your mom.' I didn't understand then that he wasn't really even my father. He was crying. He went with me and he made me wait outside in a waiting room while he went in and talked to this official for about thirty minutes. The man asked me a bunch of questions. We went through the ceremony. I raised my right hand and pledged allegiance and I was a citizen."

"I was a virgin until I got married. At my 40th high school reunion, I found out they called me the Iron Petticoat in high school. That's OK, because at that same reunion, I was approached by a woman who said she was the town whore in high school and I was the only one at school who was ever kind to her. I treated her just like everyone else. She didn't know that I was as much an outcast as she was."

Ingrid graduated from Bloomington High School in 1965 and entered Valley Community College in San Bernardino, planning to either become a physical education teacher or a kindergarten teacher.

"I loved athletics, and I loved children," she says. "I had worked at the Laurel Ivy Nursery School in Fontana before school for quite a while, arriving at 5 a.m. and working with the two and three year olds until 9 a.m., when I went to my classes at Bloomington."

Throughout her early years, Ingrid had always been a beauty with light brown hair, but after graduation, she decided

it was time for her to become the blonde she had always sensed was inside waiting to emerge.

Since then, she has lived most of her adult life as the Nordic beauty she was meant to be. Of Scandinavian and Old Norse origin, the name Ingrid means "Ing's beauty," referring to Ing, the mythical Norse god of earth's fertility who prepared the land for spring planting every year. The name Ingrid has always been popular in the royal houses of Scandinavia, and when Ingrid began wearing her sapphire blue contact lenses a couple of decades ago, she truly began to look the part of Nordic royalty.

Another parallel between the Ingrid Reeves of today and those women of the same name who came before her was the 13th century saint, Ingrid of Sweden. The first Dominican nun in Sweden, Saint Ingrid founded the first Dominican cloister there in 1281, and performed miracles that eventually led to a popular Swedish cult of her sainthood. Coincidentally, in this 21st century, her name-sake is surrounded by a spiritual aura of peace and beauty as she, too, intercedes prayerfully to help heal hurting people.

So, it was a vivacious blonde college student named Ingrid Marcus who met a handsome fellow student named Terry Street after having attended Valley Community College for a year and a half. Terry swept her off her feet. He resembled the movie actor, Robert Wagner, and even more than that, he was a good athlete. Ingrid was smitten.

"Terry was so handsome and he had the most beautiful legs," remembers Ingrid. "When he ran out onto the basket-ball court, even the guys would whistle! He was a good basketball player and he played football, too, and golf. Terry had a great personality. He was so funny. He made me laugh. I thought he was the love of my life."

Carol Proud, on the other hand, found nothing at all to laugh about when it came to Terry Street. For Carol, her friend's infatuation with Terry ended a time of great fun that she had enjoyed for more than two years.

"I'll admit it now. I was jealous," says Carol, "but I still say that Terry was 'braggy' and, in my opinion, he wasn't nearly as handsome as Ingrid thought he was."

It was 1966 and the Vietnam War was getting into full swing. Young men were being drafted into the Army every day and Terry Street was one of them. As soon as he received his draft notice, Terry rushed to join the Air Force.

Terry's younger brother, Toby, was in the Army already and he figured one "ground-pounder" in the family was enough. Besides, Toby had achieved officer status already and Terry figured that if he had to start at the bottom, he'd rather go into another branch of the military.

Ingrid was nineteen and madly in love. Terry was the man of her dreams and their marriage was going to be forever.

He was stationed at Rantoul, Illinois, awaiting deployment to Vietnam, when Ingrid drove out there to become his bride. She had been working and going to school and had earned enough money to buy herself a brand new red Chevy Malibu.

Their small wedding was held in the small base chapel at Rantoul, with both sets of parents in attendance. There was a write-up in the San Bernardino newspaper, with a photo of the bride-to-be.

Just prior to the wedding, Ingrid walked in to the base chapel sanctuary to look around. Suddenly, she became quite nauseated. Some airmen were in there setting up for the wedding ceremony, talking and cursing among themselves as young soldiers often do. When they saw her standing there, looking pale and gulping for air, they were embarrassed. They apologized profusely for their language, but she was too ill to be offended.

"Oh, I don't care," she exclaimed. "Just tell me where the ladies' room is – fast!"

Just before entering the chapel, she had been day-dreaming about this being the best day of her entire life and thinking about her "happily ever after" marriage, but now, all of a sudden, she was hit with nauseating doubt. She calmed herself down, washed her face, squared her shoulders, and emerged from the ladies' room to meet her destiny.

Looking back, Ingrid jokes that she probably should have trusted her gut instincts, but no … she's very glad she didn't. Had she not married Terry, she would not have given birth to her beautiful children, Wayne and Heidi.

"Everything happens for a reason," muses Ingrid. "It

was not meant to be a happily ever after marriage, but it was my ticket to motherhood and, amazingly, my family's ticket to a whole new way of life. If I hadn't married Terry, my 'colored' family would never have found their perfect place to blend in: Hawaii!"

As to Ingrid's "happily-ever-after" marriage to Richard Reeves, that was also in the cards. Cinderella Cheerleader was certainly destined to marry her Prince … some day in another place … once upon a time in the future.

In Aztec culture, one of the widespread beliefs is that hummingbirds, in some way, are messengers between worlds. As such, they help shamans keep nature and spirit in balance. The Cochti have a story about ancient people who lost faith in the Great Mother. In anger, she deprived them of rain for four years. The people noticed that the only creature who thrived during this drought was Hummingbird. When they studies his habits, the shamans learned that Hummingbird had a secret passageway to the underworld. Periodically, he went there to gather honey. Further study revealed that this doorway was open to Hummingbird alone because he had never lost faith in the Great Mother. This information inspired the people to regain faith. After that the Great Mother took care of them.

Chapter 3

Aloha... Hello & Goodbye

The virgin bride and her handsome airman had two lovely weeks of marital bliss before she decided it might be a good idea to check with the base hospital about a prescription for some sort of birth control.

Too late! She was already pregnant.

"I was so modest that I had put off getting my first female examination," Ingrid admits. "There I was on that cold examining table for the first time in my life. I looked up and on the ceiling there was a sign that said, 'Smile. You're on Candid Camera!' Ha! When the doctor told me I was pregnant, I really felt like I was on Candid Camera!"

Ingrid argued with the doctor, insisting it couldn't be true … she'd only been married for two weeks. He just nodded his head and smiled a Candid Camera smile. "It only takes one time," he reminded her.

Like everything else that had happened to her in her young life, Ingrid adjusted quickly to the news and was soon excited about her impending motherhood. Would she have a son or a daughter – she didn't care as long as the baby was healthy! Both families were excited at the prospect of a baby, and Terry was glad, too, although he had just gotten his orders for Vietnam and probably would not be present when Ingrid gave birth.

After Terry left for Vietnam, Ingrid went back to wait out her pregnancy at March Air Force Base near Riverside, California. It would turn out that the twenty-year-old pregnant war bride was facing her own fierce battle on the home-front.

"It was not an easy pregnancy. By the time I was seven months pregnant, my stomach was so big that I couldn't fit behind the steering wheel," recalls Ingrid. "It looked like the baby was standing up when I was lying down!"

"This can't be one baby!" declared the doctor. "There must be three in there!"

In addition to being huge with child, Ingrid was ill. She was hospitalized with toxemia for more than a month before her labor pains began . . . nearly two weeks early. Terry had just arrived on a short leave from Vietnam, to be there for the birth of his child, when Ingrid's arduous labor began. It lasted for a record fifty-four hours, with mother and infant so close to death that all of the family members were called in.

Ingrid was fighting for every breath, determined that she and her baby would live. At one point in the midst of unrelenting waves of anguish, she opened her eyes and saw, through a haze of pain, several members of Terry's family milling about the room. Doctors and nurses were there, too, and members of her family. Then she saw her dad and an admiral bending over her bed, looking down at her and talking in tones too low for her to discern.

"I must have died," she thought. "This is the way it is when you're dead."

Later, she was told that neither she nor her baby had been expected to live. There wasn't even a choice of who to save – the mother or the baby – because they were both in such dire straits. Terry, the person who would have been charged with making that terrible decision, had passed out as he watched Ingrid struggle, and been carried to another room. With multiple complications arising throughout her labor, her father, Walter Marcus, had made himself known throughout the hospital. Something had to be done to save his daughter and he would accept nothing else. Ingrid would live – period!

"My dad must have had some pull, both in the military and up above," muses Ingrid. "He had the base commander in my room and the admiral in charge of the hospital actually came in to lift up the sheets and check on me. People at the base always saluted my dad. I've never known for sure why, but he sure did know the right things to do, because Wayne and I made it!"

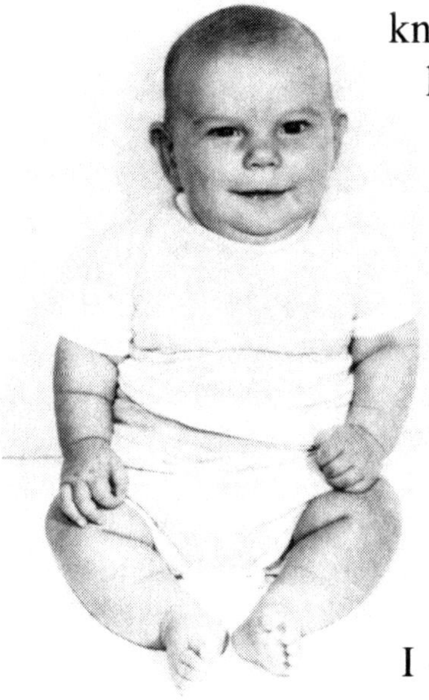

By the time Wayne Terry Street was born, on April 28, 1967, Ingrid looked like she had just crossed the Sahara Desert on foot. "My lips were cracked and dry and my hair was matted. I had been lying there thinking I was dead, and I looked like I was nearly dead. I was so exhausted that I couldn't speak and all I could think of was apples, for some reason. Then they put Wayne in my arms and nothing was ever the same again."

Weighing in at 11 pounds, 10 ½ ounces, at 21 inches long, the huge baby boy was the most gorgeous infant his mother had ever seen. "Wayne was beautiful, round and happy, with rolls of fat and dark, dark hair that washed off within a few days and turned white blonde," declares Ingrid. "He looked just like the Michelin Tire Man!"

Terry and Ingrid took their big, beautiful baby boy home to the tiny caretaker's cottage in Rialto that Ingrid had rented just months before. Within an hour of arriving home, some of Terry's Air Force buddies dropped by and Terry decided to go out for a few beers with them. "I couldn't believe he went out partying with his friends so soon after we got home, especially after the horrible struggle I'd had with the baby! I was so furious, I just turned into a gorilla!" recalls Ingrid.

"I put the baby in the bassinet and ran outside. I took my fist and hit the mailbox and knocked it to the ground. I was really strong, even after what I'd been through. I pulled branches off the trees in the yard and threw them everywhere! When they came back, it looked like a hurricane had come through that front yard. Terry got the message. He stayed home for the rest of his leave."

Three years later, on August 27, 1970, Wayne's sister, Heidi Dawn Street, was born at Kaiser Hospital in Fontana, California.

"I loved the story of Heidi and her grandfather when I was a child, and had always planned to name my daughter after that little girl on the mountain," recalls Ingrid. "I had invented a middle name for my daughter – Sunsearay – but by the time she was born, I was so exhausted, I simply named her Heidi Dawn."

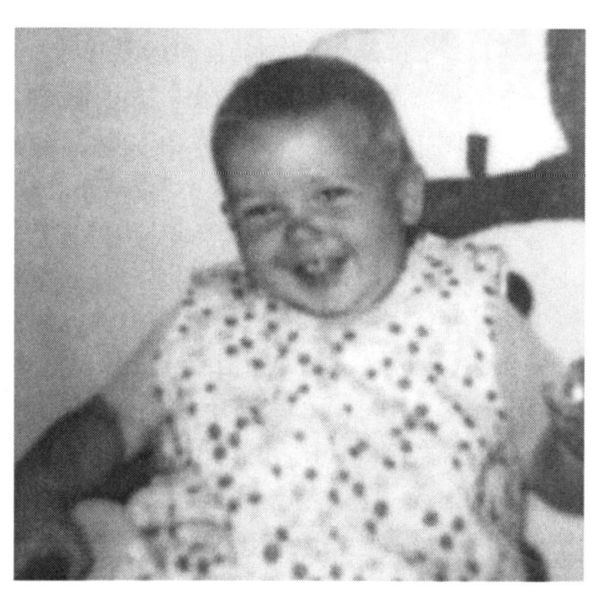

Heidi Dawn "Sunsearay" Street, Born August 27, 1970

Heidi weighed in at exactly what Wayne had weighed – 11 pounds, 10 ½ ounces – and was 23 inches long. Following Heidi's birth, the doctors insisted that Ingrid have a tubal ligation. This was necessary, they said, because the next huge baby would surely kill her.

Heidi was another plump, beautiful baby. Her hair, from the moment she was born, was so white that it sparkled. She was a tow-head until she reached high school.

At the time Heidi was born, Terry was back from his tour of duty in Vietnam and was working at Kaiser Steel Company in Fontana.

The sad circumstances of his return from Vietnam were to negatively impact Terry for the rest of his life. He and his younger brother, Toby, although in different branches of the military, had been serving simultaneously in Vietnam. The brothers were close, and had gotten together as often as they could while they were "in country."

When he heard that Toby had been injured in a fierce ground battle in Binh Dinh Province, South Vietnam, Terry had immediately initiated a relentless search for his little brother. He finally found him in an Army field hospital with part of his head blown away.

On January 18, 1969, twenty-year-old 1st Lieutenant Toby Windfield Street died the death of a decorated war hero. His brother, Airman Terry Street, lived, but a part of his heart died in that Army field hospital where he found his brother, Toby. Both brothers came back from Vietnam, never to return. Terry's tour of Vietnam was over.

"Terry came back from Vietnam a changed man," recalls Ingrid. "Rules didn't seem as important to him anymore. He would drive very fast right down the middle of the road on the line – as if he didn't care whether he lived or died. He turned into a daredevil and he wasn't afraid of anything."

Toby Street's grave site

One of four children, Terry had an older brother, Tom, and a younger sister, Tammy.

His family was totally devastated by the death of Toby, to the point that Ingrid was tasked with handling most of the calls and cards and funeral arrangements.

"I was the strong one during that period," remembers Ingrid. "Wayne was just a baby. Terry was acting wild. I had to be strong for everybody. Toby was married to Andrea and she was shattered with grief. Everybody was. I didn't cry then. I didn't have time. But years later, when I was at a poets' convention in Washington, D.C., I visited the Vietnam Wall. When I found his name, Toby Windfield Street, I just broke down and wept."

Terry and Toby's high school friend, Alexander "Sandy" Cunningham, had also gone to Vietnam, but returned before Terry was drafted. Terry was in Vietnam and Wayne was still an infant when Al "Sandy" Cunningham would regularly bring his dates by to meet Ingrid. He admired Terry's taste in women and thought so much of Ingrid that he wanted to make sure she approved of his dates. Sharon "Cher" was the one lady Sandy dated that Ingrid really liked, and he later married her.

"My first glimpse of Ingrid was at the changing table, changing Wayne's diaper," recalls Sharon "Cher" Cunningham, who has remained a close friend of Ingrid's for more than forty years.

Remembering that first time that Al (whom Ingrid has always called "Sandy") took her for Ingrid's approval, Cher says she was quite impressed with Sandy's friend. "Ingrid was so beautiful and friendly – I thought she was one of the prettiest women I'd ever met. She dressed Wayne in real cute clothes, too. He was such a fat, cute little baby and he turned out to be such a handsome man. He looks just like Tom Cruise."

Cher and Ingrid would grow into a close, comfortable friendship where they found much in common. For instance, both women especially enjoy comparing people in their lives to movie stars and celebrities – possibly because they are "California girls," and are always amazed that they are reminded of the same celebrity when they talk of a person they know.

True to form, when Cher talks of her husband, whom she calls Al but Ingrid still calls Sandy, she says he is a cross between Andy Griffith – Andy of Mayberry - and Fred McMurray – easy going, wise, slow to anger – an honest, nice, down to earth man. Sandy and Cher have remained close to Ingrid through many of life's unexpected twists and turns.

"Sandy and Cher got married on my birthday, January 24th, 1969, at a little stone church in Cucamonga. Terry and I stood up with them," recalls Ingrid, "but I didn't even realize it was my birthday until later. It was a stormy, rainy day and it was the day they were bringing Toby's body home from Vietnam. My mind and heart were storming like the weather that day. There was so much suffering – it was hard to think of anything else."

Terry's suffering went deep. In 1969, war protesters were spitting at returning soldiers and calling them killers. It was a bad time for the military and an especially bad time for Terry. He rarely talked of Vietnam, but he once shared a story with Ingrid about a wild party that he and Toby had attended when they were on R&R together. He talked dreamily of a lady they were with that night who had the most beautiful body he'd ever seen in his life. Ingrid remembers that story as her first inkling that Terry might have strayed from his marital vows, but she refused to digest that thought, or act upon it. In fact, she innocently put it aside, thinking Terry was having flash-backs to a time and place that she could never understand. Their son, Wayne, was just a toddler, after all. She would continue to comfort this troubled Vietnam veteran. She would be his tender, loving wife. This man was her forever love … this marriage was a sacred trust.

It was when she was about eight months pregnant with Heidi that she could no longer deny Terry was cheating on her.

"My brother Frank came to see me," she recalls. "I was sitting rocking in a rocking chair, very big with the baby, when Frank told me that Terry was a womanizer and had made a pass at his wife, Candy. When Terry came home, I confronted him with what Frank had said and he admitted it. I didn't know what to do. Here I was eight months pregnant with baby number two. I decided to believe Terry when he said it wouldn't happen again."

In the meantime, back at the Marcus household in Bloomington, Josephine had brought in twelve foster daughters to live at the big ranch house on the 20 acre tract of land. Ingrid's sister, Enid, who had moved back to California and lived nearby, had also taken in the maximum number of foster girls allowed by the State of California - twelve.

Possibly, Ingrid's mother had experienced a softening of her heart, but the more likely scenario was that there was money to be made with each foster child taken into a home, and there were certainly enough chores for the girls to do, especially now that Ingrid was no longer living at home. And,

seeing how her mother was faring with the foster girls, Enid had simply followed suit.

"I hated going back home to visit with Terry after Mums got the foster girls," recalls Ingrid. "He was so handsome and the girls were all over him, giving him shoulder rubs and touching him every chance they got. He didn't seem to mind it one bit, either."

Later, Ingrid was to learn that Terry had made a habit of picking up the foster girls at the bus stop and letting them do more to him than rub his shoulders.

For now, though, Ingrid simply knew that her husband was a big flirt, and it was getting harder and harder to overlook his flirting.

Soon after Heidi was born, Terry's older brother, Tom,

Grandpa William "Bill" Street, Wayne and Heidi, Terry and Grandma Maxine Street

proposed a move to Hawaii. Tom Street was manager of Pier One Imports and knew enough about Hawaii that he felt a restaurant joint venture would be successful. Terry and Ingrid jumped at the opportunity to go into a family business in Hawaii. It was a great chance to get a fresh start in an exotic new place – far from home and memories of the past."Ingrid and Terry spent the night with us right before they took off for Hawaii," recalls Cher Cunningham. "They were such a beautiful couple, with two sweet little ones … so happy, so hopeful … and yet, I remember this sneaking little thought popping into my head as we all sat around the dinner table: They're going to get a divorce."

Ingrid with Heidi and Wayne, 1970

It was strange, Cher says, because Ingrid never talked about personal things and she never seemed to let anything get her down. "The night before they left for Hawaii, it seemed they had everything going for them, but I know now that

Ingrid and I have a special bond and I must have been catching her thought waves that night."

Looking back at those days now, Ingrid finds it eerie that Cher recalls that night so vividly because she was, indeed, sitting at the dinner table pondering an uncertain future with Terry and hoping that Hawaii would be the answer to their marriage woes.

"We flew to Hawaii, sight unseen," recalls Ingrid. "It was a real adventure! We landed at the big island where the volcano is, and then went on to Maui, where we soon opened a little submarine sandwich shop called The Organ Grinder."

The Organ Grinder was almost instantly listed as one of the restaurants in the book *Hawaii on $10 a Day*, advertising the best food for the least amount of money. One reason it was a big hit right away with tourists and locals alike was that it was in one of the most interesting locations on Maui - Lahaina's Front Street.

"There was a beautiful, ornate organ grinder from Europe in the little marketplace where we rented a space," recalls Ingrid. "You could put a coin in it and there were all kinds of pipes and cymbals. There was even a whaler's tub for boiling blubber. It was a unique spot."

It didn't take much money to set up the Organ Grinder as a submarine sandwich destination – but it did take ingenuity, and that was one quality Ingrid had right at her fingertips. She had learned a great deal about thinking outside the box from working construction with her mother over the years and that know-how came in handy.

"We went to the dump and picked up a bunch of old Singer sewing machine bases – the treadle ones – and used those for the base of our tables," Ingrid remembers. "The electric company gave us some old wooden spools, which we torched and burned spots in the tops, put shells and rope around them and thick acrylic laminate to make a glossy cover for the shells. Those were our tables."

The stools were made by cutting old telephone poles to the size of a stool and putting a piece of plywood to fit on the round top, with Naugahyde™ vinyl folded beneath the plywood for the seat. They even cut out their own serving counter, where customers usually came to order the best meatball subs on the planet.

"I made three hundred meatballs every morning and by the time we closed, they were gone," grins Ingrid, recalling the hard work and the great fun of owning and working at the Organ Grinder.

Later, they opened Maui's first Mexican restaurant, The Hole in the Wall, in an old Queens Theatre that had to be closed down. "We had to go through the historic society and tell them what we were going to do, in order to locate the restaurant there," remembers Ingrid.

Cooking from scratch, Ingrid would start each day at The Hole in the Wall with a huge pot of pinto beans. She made endless burritos, something she had learned to do well in California.

"I tried making my own tortillas, but that was too much," she recalls. "We ended up ordering tortillas from the Mainland and freezing them."

The two working families – Tom and his wife, Kathy, and their 6-year old daughter, Vicky, and Terry, Ingrid, Wayne and Heidi – lived near one another at first at the brand new

Napili Apartments, sharing the cost of another old Nash Rambler to transport them back and forth from work. Later, they moved nearer to Lahaina where their two restaurants were located.

"I loved Hawaii. Wayne was three years old and Heidi was a baby. I used to take the children with me to the Organ Grinder, but first thing in the morning – right as the sun rose – I'd go surfing at Olowalu Beach."

"At dawn, Olowalu Beach was deserted. I'd make a nest cradle of towels and put baby Heidi in it on the beach, while Wayne and I went out over and over again. I'd put him on the front of my board and we'd paddle out. He still remembers it to this day."

"When the waves break and the mist flies up in the air, it's really good stuff to breath in. It's true. There's a chemical in the mist that helps surfers live longer and stay younger. If you know a surfer, you know what I mean."

"I loved chewing on seaweed, too. Terry would say, 'Stop doing that!' but I know it's really good for you."

"There are sperm whales in Hawaii very near the shore. One morning I saw the shadow of a huge whale. I put my feet on the board and there was a big eyeball right up next to me. He came up gently, didn't knock me off the board. We looked at each other eye to eye. The animals and I have always been able to communicate."

"Communicating with Terry was not as easy. He was such a flirt and it really bothered me, but I didn't say much about it.

I was working so hard and I was in charge of the children. Terry was not a doting dad. He paid more attention to the women who came into the restaurant than to the kids and me. One day I came back to the Hole in the Wall and there was a woman sitting on Terry's lap. She hopped off real quick when she saw me come in. I just kept holding in my anger at Terry. Holding it in – holding it in – until it finally exploded back in California."

"We were there at the Organ Grinder on Lahaina's Front Street Dock watching in April of 1972 when the captain of the Carthaginian ran it aground and wrecked it. It had been a 19th Century museum whaling ship and it was on its way to Honolulu for dry dock. We all knew he was going to run it aground –we told him he would, and he did!"

The sinking of the Carthaginian II

Many years later, a replica of that original whaler was built and christened the Carthaginian II. On December 13, 2005, the Carthaginian II was ceremoniously sunk in the ocean about a half mile off Lahaina's shore. Now at the bottom of the sea, about 97 feet below the surface, with the intention of the ship acting as an artificial reef. It is a beautiful attraction for both marine life and divers.

Ingrid, too, was a beautiful attraction near Lahaina's famous shore. The young, blonde Maui surfer mom named

Ingrid Street was a wonderful chef and went back and forth from the Organ Grinder to The Hole in the Wall, helping prepare food in both places. After an invigorating early morning swim, she would arrive at the Organ Grinder around 8 a.m. and get right to work while her two tow-headed little ones played in the kitchen. Later, she found a wonderful Hawaiian lady to babysit for Wayne and Heidi while she was at work.

"Mrs. Opanui had nine children. They made poi in their backyard. It was made from the taro root. I never liked poi – it tasted too much like the white paste I used to eat in elementary school because I was so hungry."

Ingrid remembers that the Opanui's had a shack with mattresses all over the floor and every morning they'd fish with huge fish nets. They would all get in a circle and round up the fish.

"It was wonderful to look at that circle around the net and spot my two little blonde children. It was a Circle of Love – quite prophetic, really."

When people asked Mrs. Opanui 'Who are those howlie babies?' she'd say, 'Those are my howlie babies!' Howlie is Hawaiian slang for Caucasian.

When they moved to Lahaina, Ingrid and her little family of four rented a storage shack from Mr. and Mrs. Wong, who were the landlords of the restaurant properties.

"They had a really nice home," she recalls, "and the storage shack where we lived was behind their big house. It was a cement-block building with a cement sink and cement floor. I gave the kids a bath in that sink. We had a regular little kitchen and bedroom and living room and bathroom. I divided the bedroom so that Heidi could have a crib, and Wayne slept in the living room. You didn't need much in Hawaii. It was warm and you spent most of your time outside, anyway."

In Hawaiian, Lahaina means "sunny spot," and it was. It could rain all over the island, but Lahaina would invariably remain dry.

One morning, Ingrid pulled up to Mrs. Opanui's on a new bicycle that she had purchased to ride to work because parking was almost non-existent in Lahaina. It had special seats to ride the children in the back. As she pulled up into the yard, Mrs. Opanui ran out yelling, "No Japanese! No Japanese bicycle! Get it out of here!" Yes, there was prejudice in Hawaii, too. Even in the racial melting pot of Hawaii, there were certain people who didn't like certain people because of race.

But Ingrid was to discover that the melting pot of Hawaii was absolutely the perfect spot for the Marcus family to blend in. Circumstances in California had made it possible for Walter and Josephine to come for a visit to Hawaii. It was to be a life-changing visit for them.

"The railroad bought out the ranch house property where my mother had taken in the twelve foster girls, and they bought it for a very good price. Mums and Dad moved to San Clemente and built a beautiful home there," says Ingrid, remembering that because San Clemente was such an exclusive area, her dad had to purchase the property alone, without her mother being there. "If they had seen my mother, they wouldn't have sold Dad the acreage."

In 1971, Walter and Josephine Marcus had their new

home in San Clemente, and no longer had a house full of foster girls. It was then that they decided to take a nice vacation to Hawaii and visit Ingrid and Terry and the kids. "Mums loved it. She fit in on Maui. Everyone thought she was Hawaiian. They mistook her for Filipino or Chinese or a mix of both – but she just really looked like the islander she was. Because my sister, Enid, looked just like Mums, she fit in, too. No one in Hawaii was at all prejudiced against them. It was a new feeling, especially for Enid. It didn't take long for them to decide to stay."

Looking back, Ingrid marvels that, once again, she ended up being the outcast. "My family and Hawaii were a perfect match, but I was the howlie!" she exclaims.

"I started the Marcus migration to Hawaii, but it didn't matter who my family was or what they looked like. The natives were prejudiced against me because I was Caucasian. It was even hard for a Caucasian to open a restaurant. We were not welcome. We were treated just like blacks were treated in New York back then."

Nearly everyone in the Marcus family who came to visit Ingrid and Terry ended up living in Hawaii. But, even today, in the enlightened twenty-first century society of the islands, when Ingrid goes to a family graduation or wedding, she is still asked by Hawaiians if she is "the real Auntie!"

Both the Organ Grinder and the Hole in the Wall restaurants were doing very well in 1972, but Ingrid began noticing that she and Terry were seeing none of the profits.

"Tom and Kathy could afford to send Vicky to a private school and we couldn't afford to send Wayne to the same school. We were supposed to be equal partners, but they seemed to be making all the money. I asked Terry, 'How in the world can they afford to live in a beautiful condo while we're still living in this cement storage shed?' "

Finally, Ingrid decided to confront Tom. "Are you embezzling money from us?" she asked him.

"He looked me right in the eye and said yes."

After that, they split up. Terry and Ingrid got the Organ Grinder and the partners sold the Hole in the Wall.

"Besides being broke, Terry and I were both hurt by what Tom had done. Our hearts just weren't in the restaurant business anymore, and to top it off, Wayne was ready to start school and we were concerned about the school system in Hawaii. It was time for us to go home."

At about that same time, Josephine and Walter had decided to stay on Maui permanently, so Ingrid and Terry simply gave them the Organ Grinder as a gift, and headed back to California for another fresh start.

Heidi was two years old and Wayne was five when they moved to Sacramento. That first Christmas, Terry and Ingrid took their two blonde little kids to see Santa Claus. Had Ingrid had the opportunity to sit on Santa's lap, she would surely have asked him to bring her family a happier new life than the one they had left behind in Hawaii.

After moving into a tiny apartment, Terry and Ingrid came to an agreement about the future. Terry had always wanted to try his hand at being a professional golfer and they decided that this was the time. Ingrid promised to work for a year and support the family while Terry attended college and pursued his dream of being a pro golfer.

"I immediately got a job as a waitress at the Carousel Restaurant at a mall in Sacramento," said Ingrid. "I loved my job. I was a people person and made great tips. Terry golfed every day and went to Sacramento College on the GI Bill. It was a good plan. He had a real passion for golf and he won a lot of amateur golf tournaments, but it was clear pretty soon that he would never be a professional. He couldn't seem to stay away from the 19th hole."

For nearly a year, they lived on the money Ingrid made as a waitress. Ingrid rode a bicycle to work, dropped Heidi off at a babysitter's house and took Wayne to kindergarten.

"After a year, we moved back to Rialto to be closer to Terry's parents. We rented the cutest little house there. I talked the lady into giving it to me for about $200 a month because that's all I could afford. Heidi was three, Wayne was nearly six and my marriage to Terry was nearly over."

"It was New Year's Eve, 1972, and we were at a party at Sandy and Cher's house. We all had little kids back then and we'd put the babies in the bedroom and party in the living room - it was all any of us could afford. That New Year's Eve, Terry's

flirting got to me more than ever before. It was a turning point in my heart, where I just finally decided I'd had enough. It was after that night that I really started accepting things I'd heard about Terry and other women – things that I just couldn't ignore any longer."

"When I told Terry I wanted a divorce, he didn't even argue. He didn't deny anything or ask for custody of the children or anything. He just didn't seem to care. I cared a lot. I was heartbroken. As hard as I had tried, my happily-forever-after marriage was just not to be."

"Terry's parents were really supportive. They loved Wayne and Heidi so much. I was glad they cared, because there was one day when I stopped being the strong one. Everything seemed to come down on me at once, and I didn't feel like living anymore. I dropped the kids off with Terry's parents and drove to the freeway overpass. I was actually standing there looking down at the freeway, imagining falling headfirst like I did from that elm tree back when I was eight years old, except this time I'd be falling into traffic. I was leaning way forward over the rail when I saw their van. There were Terry's parents with my kids in their van and I thought, 'Oh my God, What am I doing? Who's going to end up taking care of my children? I can't do this!'"

"Terry moved back to Hawaii after we got divorced and actually went back into business with his brother, Tom. Can you believe it? They owned Blue Water Properties in Princeville, Kawai – a real estate business. He was supposed to send me $75 a month for each of our children, but he never did. The kids ended up visiting him over there sometimes as

they were growing up, but I'm so glad that I didn't leave them motherless that day on the freeway overpass. Their lives would have been very different – that's for sure!"

"I was lucky with babysitters. I actually found another lady with nine kids to take care of my children. She was a Mexican lady from Mexico City and she babysat for me in Rialto for a really reasonable fee."

"After the divorce, Terry's parents and his sister, Tammy, also helped me with the kids. Tamala Wein Street was a gem and she was Wayne and Heidi's special Aunt Tammy. She worked at the Veterans Hospital at Loma Linda in the eyes, ears, nose and throat department and it was there that she caught a terrible case of pneumonia. She was just thirty years old when she died on September 26, 1984. The kids and I loved her very much."

"I went back to work for Rapid Color in Glendale after Terry and I were divorced. I had worked for them while he was in Vietnam, too, until I couldn't fit behind the steering wheel. They were film developers for Martin Luther King Hospital, Jet Propulsion Laboratories, Howard Hughes Aircraft, and some government agencies. My job was quality control and I had to be bonded to look at the photos. They called me "The Hawk" because I could see the slightest thing that was wrong with a print – whether it needed a color correction – what was wrong with it. What I did then is now a lost art."

"I saw some horrific stuff at Rapid Color – some photos of burn victims and some Vietnam photos and crime scenes that I'll never forget. Some of them were just awful. I'd smile and

laugh on the outside, but a lot of that stuff did get to me. There was one little five-year-old girl whose body was so severely burned she looked like a melted candle – only her face was untouched – she was so beautiful from the head up and her poor little body was so awful, it made me cry. I went home and hugged my two beautiful children, and I wondered what our future would be."

Then, one August day in 1973, Ingrid's future came into much clearer focus. She went to dinner at Club 66 in Cucamonga and met her soul mate, Richard Reeves. He turned out to be the *true* happily-ever-after man of her dreams.

Richard Reeves and Ingrid Marcus Street were both young divorcees with two children each. Both were avid athletes, both loved to dance, golf, camp, hunt and fish, both enjoyed taking their children to Disneyland and Magic Mountain, and neither of them were the least bit afraid of hard work.

Little did the attractive young couple suspect, as they took their first graceful turn around the dance floor at Club 66, that they were destined to build a fabulous life together on their own magic mountain.

Maya Hummingbird Love Lore

In days so long ago the god Baalam Kej, known as the Jaguar-Deer, transformed into a hummingbird so that he could escape the jealousy of the father of the Lady Moon. Unaware of this transformation the Lady Moon came upon a hummingbird while retrieving water from the stream. This hummingbird was such a lovely sight to see, with vivid and brilliant colors. Lady Moon was drawn so magically to this hummingbird, entranced by its beauty and grace. The hummingbird showed no fear and allowed itself to be captured. Lady Moon carefully put the hummingbird within her blouse, nestled between her breasts, and carried the hummingbird home.

Lady Moon's father, Qaawa' Tzuul Taq'a, known as the creator and supreme god, was thrilled that his daughter was so happy, and so he built her a house for her hummingbird. The house was placed within Lady Moon's sleeping quarters. How wonderful for Baalam Kej, for here he was in the form of the hummingbird, and he gained access to the bedroom of his beloved Lady Moon. Later that night they eloped. Since that time the daytime, Jaguar-Deer, the sun-god and the moon goddess are the match made in heaven, continuing day and night since the beginning of time.

Chapter 4

The Journey to Magic Mountain

While rummaging through old photos and newspaper clippings one day in 2010, Ingrid glanced at an old newspaper clipping from 1964 … and then she looked again. There was Richard Reeves, the champion Fontana High School wrestler, on one side of the page, and Bloomington High School's Ingrid Marcus of the GAA on the other side!

"Richard's mother was so proud of her son, the wrestler, when she gave me that clipping years after we were married, and when I turned it over and saw myself, I just laughed. I'm sure my mother would never have saved the newspaper clipping of me, and she definitely wouldn't have bragged about it years later," said Ingrid.

Regardless of the differences and the similarities between the two teens in the two nearby high schools, sharing the same sports page was surely a harbinger of things to come. It was almost as if Richard and Ingrid had to be groomed by life before they could meet, because Ingrid remembers it as love at first sight and is pretty sure she would have loved

Richard instantly if she had ever laid eyes on him in high school.

Even their life experiences leading up to that meeting at Club 66 were somewhat parallel, particularly from high school on, with Richard graduating from Fontana High School in 1964 and Ingrid graduating from Bloomington High School in 1965. Both attended nearby community colleges and then both were caught up in the Vietnam War. Like Terry, Richard had been drafted and had immediately joined the Navy, his chosen branch of the military. Richard had been deployed to Vietnam between 1966 and 1969 and, before his marriage to Kitty ended in 1972, had fathered two children, Jason and Christian. Ingrid and her two children and Richard and his two children were soon spending a lot of time together.

Ingrid at
Magic Mountain, 1973

"One of the first things I noticed about Richard was his willingness to help with the children," recalls Ingrid. "Terry wouldn't change a diaper and used to call me at work to come home and feed the baby. Richard knew what to do with the children and he did it. Whether we were going camping or over to someone's house for a visit, he'd have the kids packed up and ready by the time I got ready to go. It was wonderful!"

It was a good thing that Richard knew what to do with children because, as Ingrid laughingly recalls, they usually had about eight kids with them when they went anywhere – nieces and nephews as well as their own – especially when they went camping, which was nearly every weekend. Richard's mother was back in Oklahoma when he met Ingrid, but his sister, Barbara, lived in Costa Mesa, California, and her boys, David and Ricky, were usually part of the young entourage accompanying Richard and Ingrid on their adventures.

Christian, Heidi, Jason and cousin Ricky

"We'd bought an old bread truck and a motor home, both for under $500, and used those to go camping with the kids nearly every weekend. We always had a slew of kids with us any time we went anywhere – even Disneyland or Magic Mountain," recalls Ingrid.

There was one day early in their relationship when they took a bread-truck-load of kids to Magic Mountain in

Valencia. Richard was in charge of the older ones, and Ingrid had two-year-old Chris and three-year-old Heidi by the hand as they walked through a candy shop and other attractions, eventually stopping at a game that involved throwing dimes on a plate. In search of dimes, Ingrid dropped Chris's hand for a split second and he was gone. They reported him to the lost and found. As time dragged on and Chris was still missing, the group got panicky. It was when they decided to retrace their steps that they found Chris, sitting happily on a tall chair in the candy shop with a huge swirly sucker. Ingrid was amazed. "At age two, Chris knew exactly where that candy shop was and the lady in there rewarded him with a big sucker instead of taking him to the lost and found."

Chris was a charmer at age two and, according to his devoted step-mother, continues to be a charmer today. "He was a beautiful child – very blonde, blue-eyed – the type that everyone adored. Chris could get away with just about anything," says Ingrid. "He looked just like Richard as a child. He was a charismatic cutie, and a very adventurous

little boy, like his big brother, Jason. Jason was mechanically inclined from the start. He was constantly creating rockets out of balsa wood and shooting them off with little engines into space."

Ingrid got to know Richard and his boys very well during their first few months together, as they spent a great deal of time camping in the wilderness.

"We loved camping and hiking and fishing and hunting. We were young and strong and tough – the outdoors was where we functioned best."

It was in the wilderness that they bonded, sharing bits and pieces of their childhood memories and getting comfortable with their similar lifestyle philosophies. Although Richard had faced many challenges as a child, he was quicker to talk about his childhood than Ingrid was to talk about hers.

Richard and his dad Otto

She had been too well-trained for too many years to reveal much – at least for a while.

Richard was born in West Los Angeles, California on May 7, 1945. He spent his childhood going back and forth between Long Beach and Fontana, California, and Tulsa, Oklahoma, where his mother, Kathryn Carter Reeves, had relatives. When he was nine years old, his father, Otto Carroll Reeves, died of a heart attack in Tulsa, Oklahoma.

That same year, Richard was one of the first open heart surgery patients in Tulsa, due to his congenital heart condition, patent ductus arteriosus –PDA (sometimes referred to as blue baby syndrome). Doctors had told his family that nine-year-old Richard had the heartbeat of an eighteen-year-old. They warned his mother that the boy would never be strong and would be unable to participate in competitive sports. The doctors were wrong. Richard went out for wrestling and water polo at Fontana High School and became a wrestling champion. He later won top honors in mixed martial arts in the Navy on board the USS Winston (AKA-94/LKA-94), an Andromeda Class attack cargo ship.

A vigorous, self-sufficient man who made his own way in the world through hard work and a powerful combination of brain and brawn, Richard Reeves had finally met his match in Ingrid.

Ingrid and Richard spent more time doing things with their children than they did doing things as a couple, but their first date following their meeting at Club 66 was a golf date at the Ontario Golf Course.

"Richard didn't know how to spell my first name," laughs Ingrid. "He said, 'OK, you fill out the score card,'

and thought I wouldn't catch on, but I did." In addition to enjoying a good laugh together, the couple found they were as well-matched on the golf course as they were on the dance floor.

"Richard was a good dancer," she recalls. "That's back when disco was popular and we went dancing at the Fontana Inn several times, but mainly, we were with the kids and going to family functions or camping."

Most of Ingrid's family was in Hawaii by that time, with the exception of her older sister Dee, who was in Glendale. Sometimes, they'd visit Dee. And, one day, after about two years of avoiding her old friends, Sandy and Cher, Ingrid decided she would drop by and see them.

"I hadn't wanted to say anything negative about Terry, so I guess that's why I let the time slip by," says Ingrid. "Then I just thought to myself, 'I miss Cher. I want to keep being her friend.'"

"Ingrid is truly like a real-life Mary Poppins," declares Cher. "Life is never boring when she's around. I was so happy when she pulled up, out of the blue, driving some kind of an old bread truck! It was a real fluke, because at that very moment, my son, Justin, was so sick that I was heading out the door to take him to the hospital. Ingrid went with us."

Cher remembers that Justin was about two years old and was screaming and crying so hard that he was just about uncontrollable. When they were led to a waiting room with a rocking chair in it, Ingrid sat down in it and said, "Let me have that baby." Almost instantly, the child calmed down.

"After that day, Justin was in love with Ingrid," recalls Cher. "He called her EENRID. He'd say, 'Where's

EENRID?' constantly, and when he saw her, he was thrilled! We never knew when we'd see her after that. Ingrid would just drop by unannounced. She'd say, 'I just dropped Richard off at the airport – do you want some company?'"

Cher had an old player piano and the two friends would play and sing honky tonk tunes and drink Ingrid's original concoction that she called Yucca Blossoms (made in a blender with frozen limeaid, rum and coconut snow). "It was always a fun adventure when 'EENRID' showed up," recalls Cher, grinning. "We had a ball, singing and playing the piano. We even made a crazy tape of our songs one time. We still see each other and keep in touch. Even if a year or two passes between visits, it's like we just saw each other yesterday. I know we'll go to our graves being best friends."

For Ingrid, renewing old friendships was a turning point and her new relationship with Richard, hopefully, pointed to a new path toward permanent happiness.

"When I met Richard, he was working at Sunkist Orange Juice Company," says Ingrid. "He had taken Mechanical Engineering at Chaffee College in Rancho Cucamonga, and during high school, he had been so advanced that he had worked for the City of Fontana as a drafter. Richard was very smart and I knew he had a great future ahead of him. I knew I wanted to be there to help make it happen and to share that future with him, but we were both so afraid of commitment. Two failed marriages made us very hesitant about going through another marriage ceremony any time soon."

In fact, as if to demonstrate his lack of true commitment to their relationship, some months after they began dating Richard left Sunkist and moved to Reno, Nevada, to accept a job as a drafter with a company there. He had been in Reno for a couple of months when Ingrid decided to take a trip up there to see him. She left the kids with the Mexican lady that had nine children, and flew to find out how Richard was faring in Reno without her.

"I'd seen flashes of Richard in my head. My heart told me we were supposed to be together. I missed him so much. I didn't realize it at the time, but I was actually going there to rescue him from that gambling town and bring him home to us. Once he saw me, he realized he didn't want to stay there anymore. I had flown into Reno alone, but we drove back together in his little Volkswagen that we had nicknamed *Herbie, the Love Bug*."

Ingrid's two children were always with them, but

Richard had custody of his two only during the summer and on some holidays. During the winter months, Jason and Christian stayed with their mother in San Bernardino. "From the beginning, no matter where they were at the moment, Jason and Christian were like my own children," says Ingrid, "and Richard treated Wayne and Heidi like his own, too."

Richard and Ingrid began living together in 1974, moving to Glendale and renting a little caretaker's cottage on an unspoiled acre of land in the middle of the city. "Every morning, there were deer on the front lawn. There were avocado trees and Chinese fruit trees – it was like a little country oasis in the middle of town," recalls Ingrid. "We had Heidi and Wayne with us all the time and we got Jason and Christian as often as we could – summers and holidays, for sure. We loved taking the kids to Santa Monica Pier, fishing. You could stay out there all night long. You can't do that anymore."

By the time they were twelve years old, both Jason and Christian had been granted permission by the court to be permanently in the custody of their father and step-mother.

They also lived in Hacienda Heights for a while. Ingrid was working two jobs, as a grocery clerk at Alpha Beta Grocery Store and as a cocktail waitress at a brand new restaurant called Cattleman's Wharf.

"I dressed up like a little French maid," she recalls. Richard was working long hours as a mechanical engineer. They were struggling not only to pay the bills but to save up as much money as they could because they wanted to buy some property up in the Southern California hills.

Their mutual love of the California wilderness was

shared and inspired by Richard's beloved uncle, Wyatt Carter, who led the way by moving out to the hills first. Uncle Wyatt, an old Navy sailor who had survived Pearl Harbor, was Richard's father figure and a fine figure of a man, despite the fact that he had become a paraplegic in a jeep accident. When Kathryn Reeves was left a widow with three children to raise (Richard and his two sisters, Barbara and Caroline), her eight brothers had rallied around her as much as possible. Her brother, Wyatt, had a special place in his heart for young Richard and did all he could to ease his fatherless nephew's pain as he grew to manhood.

When Wyatt and his wife, Ama Jane "Janie," bought some property in the hills of Nuevo, Richard and Ingrid helped them move from Seal Beach to their new place. When she first saw Janie, Ingrid remembers that she was

Uncle Wyatt Carter and Jane Carter

amazed at her beauty.

"She was stunning! She had the most beautiful grey eyes, and she was a marvelous cook," says Ingrid. "The way they met was interesting, too. They were both champion archers. Wyatt's upper body strength was incredible and he was so good that he could split an arrow. He had a sharp sense of humor, too. When they first met, he and Janie had both been married to other people, but they left those other people and married each other. Wyatt always joked that he and Janie 'split the sheets.'"

When Wyatt and Janie decided to move from Seal Beach, California, to the hills of Nuevo, Richard and Ingrid offered to help and almost instantly fell in love with the area themselves.

"We were sitting on a boulder looking out at their little five-acre farm when we saw some weeds moving right next to their place. There was a mountain lion with her three cubs, right there. It was magical. I always noticed the wildlife. I was drawn to the animals … still am."

Wyatt and Janie fixed up a nice little farm with a pond and geese and chickens and rabbits. He had a little tractor – actually an ATV Quad that Richard had fixed up for him to work with hand controls – and every time he started it up, all the animals would come. He would drive it down to feed the ducks and chickens and rabbits and if he wasn't right on time, the animals would come up the hill to get him.

Looking at the stars from that vantage point was one of the attractions for the young couple, too, and Richard credited Wyatt with inspiring him to be a star-gazer at a very young age. Wyatt had a great little telescope and was constantly peering at the heavens.

One day, though, Ingrid noticed that Wyatt had the telescope aimed a bit lower and was concentrating intently.

"What in the world are you looking at, Wyatt?" she asked. He just grinned and offered to let her check out the view. "There was a nudist colony down there," she recalls. "The telescope was powerful enough that we could see the naked people swimming around in the pool and diving from the diving board!"

Wyatt thoroughly enjoyed life, despite his injury. He always said, after they moved to Nuevo, that Richard had given him back his "legs" when he custom-built the ATV-tractor so that he could maneuver it and go exploring in the hills. Once, when Ingrid asked Wyatt what he missed most as a paraplegic, he got very quiet and responded, with a sad sigh, "dancing."

Wyatt Carter and Aunt Betty Reeves

As one who has loved to dance all of her life, Ingrid was especially touched by that statement. "Since that moment, every time I've danced, I've danced for Uncle Wyatt as well as for myself."

Richard and Ingrid loved coming to Nuevo to visit with Wyatt and Janie and soon decided it was time to spend some of their hard-earned money on buying some nearby property.

Their first twenty acres would eventually grow to an eighty-four-acre mountain that rose to a pinnacle of 2,500 feet. Together, they envisioned becoming one with the mountain and the wildlife it supports, but as the early settlers did before them, they had to clear some of the land in order to make it habitable.

"We came home from work every day and worked on clearing the land," Ingrid remembers. "There were huge boulders all over the property and a mile of dirt road to be cleared. We paid every extra dime we had to the dozer and dynamite men."

It was Ingrid's job to help Boom Boom Fuller, the dynamite man.

"Mr. Fuller was a huge man. It was just the two of us. We had to take all the equipment – drills and hoses and dynamite and water jugs to put out the fires he started with the dynamite. He'd drill the hole – the heat was terrific – we'd drag all those hoses and drills up the hill, put the dynamite in there, stuff it like a sausage, then he'd put in those charges and go down the hill a bit and set off the charge. Mr. Fuller would always say, 'When I set this charge off, rocks will come at you like baseballs. Just avoid them.' I did avoid them. I was quick.

Mr. Fuller had a cute little dog – a wire-haired fox terrier - that would run to the dynamite hole and sniff it – and then the dozer man would come and move all the rocks and Mr. Fuller and I would move on to the next hill of boulders."

Every time Wyatt drove his ATV over the hill and saw Richard and Ingrid together, he'd warn Richard that he'd better marry Ingrid.

"Don't let this one get away," he repeatedly told

Richard. "If you don't marry her, I'm going to marry her!"

Finally, on May 20, 1977, Richard and Ingrid were married at the courthouse in Riverside, California. Wyatt and Janie stood up with them, and the wedding party returned to Nuevo. Then it was time for the newlyweds to return to their own Magic Mountain and move more boulders.

When Richard's beloved Uncle Wyatt – William Wyatt Carter, Jr. – passed away on May 31, 1996 in Seal Beach, California, Ingrid wrote the following poem in tribute to his extraordinary life:

UNCLE WYATT

Standing proud as witness on our very special wedding day,
what a wonderful moment when you gave the bride away.
Our children learning, as you taught them the game of chess
– hours spent playing to see which one was the best.
Rides through wondrous desert mountains,
we all loved so dearly.
Rabbits scampering amongst the quail, rattlesnakes and
other mountain creatures,
oh but Uncle Wyatt you were our teacher.
Always there when needed, in glad times and sad times.
Quiet times spent feeding the birds,
Ducks come a-running when Wyatt's tractor they heard.
Wyatt, you will always be in our thoughts and hearts forever.
With hands like a vise! A heart of gold!
Friendship, love, and guiding advice ...We miss you!
(As Wyatt would always lovingly say,
"I am glad you got to see me.")
Love forever,
Ingrid Yvette Reeves

Aztec Hummingbird Lore

The Aztecs came to believe that every warrior
slain in battle rose to the sky
and orbited the sun for four years.
Then they became hummingbirds.
In the afterlife these transformed heroes
fed on the flowers in the gardens of paradise,
while engaging from time to time
in mock battles to sharpen their skills.
At night the hummingbird angels
became soldiers again and followed Huitzil,
fighting off the powers of the darkness,
restoring warmth and light.
The sun rewarded them for this by giving them
a radiant sheen.

In an Aztec ritual, dancers formed a circle
and sang a song which included these words:

"I am the Shining One, bird, warrior and wizard."

At the end of the ritual young men lifted young girls,
helping them to fly like hummingbirds.

Chapter 5

Triple R Ranch... Reeves, Rocks & Rattlesnakes

Yes, rattlesnakes!

"We killed one-hundred and twenty-one (121) rattlesnakes the first year we lived on the mountain," Ingrid states somewhat matter-of-factly. "Nowadays, we only kill about five a year."

Taking up residence in Homeland, California, at what came to be called the "Triple R" (Reeves, Rocks & Rattlesnakes) was akin to taking a step back in time. It was as if the Reeves were a family of modern day pioneers ... time travelers taking daily leaps between two distinct lifestyles – the present and the past.

In the present, Ingrid and Richard were struggling to make ends meet, working hard to provide for the needs of their large blended family. Each of them drove off early every morning to work at full-time jobs at modern, air-conditioned plants.

Richard worked in Riverside as the superintendent at E. C. DeYoung – Power Replacements, a firm that built test cells for jet airplane engines. Ingrid worked in the Alumax factory in Riverside, building aluminum siding for mobile homes by day, and working part-time some nights and weekends as a hostess at Massacre Canyon, a nearby golf course that featured a dinner club.

Wayne and Heidi (and later, Jason and Christian) attended public schools, made good grades, were active in sports, and regularly traveled by airplane and automobile to spend time with their respective "other parents."

At the end of long hours at work and school, the Reeves family returned home to a simpler time and place, traveling back in time and living almost like 18th century California pioneers at their remote home in the wilderness. There, they were totally "off the grid" and about as far removed as they could be from the modern amenities enjoyed by most of the citizens of the United States in the late 1970s.

"We wanted the simple life, with old-fashioned values, no frills and no big city stuff," says Ingrid. "We moved far out because we wanted to live and raise our children in the country, in the wide open spaces where we could go hiking and watch the stars and take time to listen to the music of the wind."

Before buying the boulder-strewn mountain in their home state of California, they had even considered moving to Oregon or some other remote, unspoiled place in the country but, thanks to Uncle Wyatt and Janie, they found the unique way of life they sought right in their own backyard.

"Breathtakingly beautiful, wild, lovely, natural,

pristine ..." all of those words and more flooded their minds and hearts the day Richard and Ingrid sat on a boulder in nearby Nuevo and watched a mountain lion and her three cubs.

This incredible untamed land of mountain lions and building sized boulders beckoned them that day and they began searching for the place that would be theirs alone. They didn't want to take it away from the mountain lion and her cubs, rather to harmoniously share it with them.

Being "off the grid" began more as a financial than a philosophical act for Richard and Ingrid. In addition to spending every spare dime on dynamite and dozers to clear the land and pay for more acreage, they were literally, "at the end of the road," far away from any of the electric or utility services provided by Riverside County.

Philosophically, life had taught both Richard and Ingrid to be self-reliant survivors, and they wanted their children to learn the value of hard work and independent thinking. While they focused on building a solid life for their family, they continually increased their land holdings and their access to modern conveniences that were financially impossible, but doable with ingenuity.

It would be twelve years before the Reeves family could afford to be "on the grid." In some respects, they are remembered as the best twelve years of their lives.

For the first five years on the property, until they purchased a double-wide trailer from Richard's cousins, the family resided in a makeshift campsite that consisted of the bread truck and the Terry travel trailer that they had previously taken camping. Now, they camped out for real!

The kids slept in the bread truck, where there was a big

bunk above and two beds to the side. Ingrid and Richard slept in the Terry travel trailer and Richard built a little lean-to outside the trailer with corrugated, fiberglass roofing material. Beneath the lean-to was a bathtub. At first, pots of water were boiled on the wood-burning stove and the tub was filled daily for bathing. Then Richard rigged up a solar heating panel on top of the Terry travel trailer to heat water for the shower. Water was used sparingly, as it had to be hauled in.

"The Old Grey Mare"
(the original bread truck where the children slept)

Heidi remembers that the morning ritual of washing their faces and brushing their teeth was strictly supervised by Ingrid.

"It was always in the same order – the oldest to the

youngest – first Wayne, then Jason, then me and then poor Chris. By the time it got to him, the water was pretty well used."

"Water was as precious as gold to us," Ingrid says. "For two years, we hauled our water in a $100 water wagon from a place about five miles away called The Water Hole that was owned by the county. The water truck held about five hundred gallons of water and we brought it back to a galvanized water tank that we had paid about $25 for."

Generally, they tried to keep the water tank about one thousand gallons full. They also had barrels and deep dozer-dug ponds all over the place to catch any rainwater, although the rainy season is extremely short in that part of California.

When they showered in the little Terry travel trailer and even later, when they had an actual shower inside the double-wide, there was a definite shower regimen observed by all.

"There was a five minute shower time," recalls Ingrid. "No longer than five minutes." Ingrid recalls the strictly enforced shower routine:

1) Get wet
2) Turn off the water
3) Soap your body from head to toe
4) Turn on the water
5) Rinse off and turn off the water.

Part of the shower ritual included the placement of a bucket on the floor to catch water run-off. The water in the bucket was then used to flush the toilet.

Although Richard would later design and engineer an extremely efficient sewer system, and the family would help him build it, there was only a septic tank at first. One of the daily chores for the two older boys was to empty and dispose of the contents of the septic tank located beneath the bathroom in the trailer. Filling a K-Mart "blue bag" with the contents of the septic tank, the boys would trek to a remote burial spot at least once a day.

"When we had company, we made more than one 'blue bag' trip," recalls Wayne, noting that those early days of "blue bag" latrine duty went a long way in preparing him for his later stint in the infantry.

"I hear water!" Ingrid whispered to Richard one day as they were hiking up a hill on their property. "Shhhh . . . listen!" It was sweet mountain music, indeed. About five acres up from their valley home, a natural rock spring gurgled merrily away.

"We had hauled water for nearly two years before we found that wonderful spring. We tapped into it with hoses and brought the water down to the tank."

The rock spring had clear, sweet water in it even when there had been no rain for months. Now they knew why the property below the Triple R Ranch was called the Rock Springs Ranch.

Ingrid's rock spring was their main source of water until they decided, about eight years later, that it was time to drill a well.

"We had an old Scout jeep and we traded it to a couple of guys who drilled us a well. We bartered for many things, and we lived off the land as much as we possibly could."

In addition to keeping rabbits and chickens, and sometimes pigs and goats for food, the Reeves were avid hunters and fishermen.

Wildlife of many varieties abounds on the mountain and the family hunted rabbit, deer and quail. With the ocean just one hour from the mountain, Santa Monica Pier was still a regular fishing destination for catching fish and spider crabs and setting lobster traps. “Once we caught a giant squid!” declares Ingrid. “I made squid jerky.”

She made jerky out of a lot of different game, especially venison, drying it on one of her three cast-iron wood-burning stoves.

“We used two of the stoves for heating and one for cooking,” recalls Ingrid, “but I could and did cook on all three of them. Richard and I love antiques and we found a great place in Fallbrook, California, that sold nothing but old wood burning stoves at reasonable prices. The Stove Man was a huge barn loaded with leftover wood-burners from the 1800s and early 1900s.”

One day, Ingrid found a black cast-iron antique cook stove at The Stove Man for around $200. She was in the process of buying it when all of a sudden, Richard shouted from the back of the barn, “Ingrid, wait a minute.” Rooting around behind all the other stoves, Richard had found a beautiful blue wood-burning cook stove with porcelain hearts for handles.

“It was aqua blue, like the ocean, and that’s the one we bought. I cooked on it for years and still own it,” says Ingrid, “but that wasn’t the last I ever saw of that pretty old black cast iron stove I was looking at first. There were some other people trying to buy it at the same time I was and they were from the Nixon Library. Sure enough, years later, we went to a family wedding at the Nixon Library and there was the very same old cook stove that I almost bought."

The aqua-blue wood-burning cook stove with the heart handles was exactly right for the surfer girl turned pioneer woman who was the heart of the Reeves family.

Ingrid was destined to add a special ingredient called love to every meal she cooked on the stove. In fact, Ingrid's creative flair combined with the native wood that was used to fire up the stove was a flavor enhancer that would have been the envy of the finest restaurant.

Ingrid's home style, old-fashioned cooking was definitely augmented by the quality of the native wood, laurel sumac – that was used in the cook stove. Laurel sumac, sometimes called a sugar bush, is an evergreen hardwood that grows wild everywhere on the Reeves' mountain. The wood has many oils in it and is highly flammable. It has deep green, very thick leaves and is slow growing.

"At first, we thought it was mesquite," says Ingrid, "but the sugar bush only grows to be about twelve feet tall and when in full bloom, there are tiny furry berries on it. The animals eat the berries."

A thick vine grows at the bottom of the laurel sumac. On the vine is a green pod with thorns on it that is called a chaparral cucumber. The vine winds its way over the entire tree, symbiotic in that it keeps the tree watered through the cucumbers. The underbrush and vine were mainly the wood that was gathered for Ingrid's stove, burning sweetly, flavoring and tenderizing everything prepared there.

In addition to providing the fuel for cooking, the larger laurel sumacs made good shade trees. "I trimmed them in the shape of an umbrella and the dark green leaves made a great canopy," Ingrid recalls.

Ingrid enjoyed the entire process of sending the kids out to gather fire-wood and then rewarding them with the best treat of all . . . chocolate chip cookies. When she was about to begin mixing Toll House™ cookie dough from scratch, Ingrid would send the children out for two eggs.

"I remember one day Heidi came running in with eggs that were still soft – the shell had not hardened yet and they were just the membrane. It was the first time I realized that the shell hardened later. Those were the freshest eggs ever, and they made the cookies even better!"

It wasn't easy to maintain a steady temperature on the wood burning stove, but Ingrid managed to do it. "The cookies had to be watched every minute, but they were worth it. Those cookies were soft-bake and they came out just perfectly. Everything I cooked back then, including the cookies, had a delicious flavor that can't be duplicated on a regular modern stove."

Firing up that ocean-blue wood-burning stove with the heart handles was an act of love with which Ingrid started her day, every day, at 5 a.m. Early rising was the habit of a lifetime for Ingrid. As in childhood, it remained a necessity.

Ingrid cooked a full breakfast for the family, sometimes grilling ham, cheese and bread in a special open toasting contraption that turned out what looked like grilled cheese sandwiches, and sometimes cooking bacon and eggs and biscuits and hash-browns.

"I'd grate the potatoes on the hand grater, wash the starch off of them and make hashbrowns," she recalls. "We had chickens for the eggs, and, sometimes, pigs for the bacon and ham, but we bought flour, potatoes and milk – mostly powdered milk, which I mixed with cold water from the refrigerator."

Yes, refrigerator. They actually had three propane-powered refrigerators – one with a small freezer.

While cooking for the family was Ingrid's job, each of

the kids had their morning chores to do as well. Heidi fed the rabbits in their cages every morning, and Chris was in charge of feeding the chickens and gathering the eggs. Richard and the boys often went hunting before sun-up and came back with wild game to dress before they began dressing themselves for work and school.

"They brought me a deer one morning and I jerkied the whole thing," recalls Ingrid. "We sliced it very thin and I put all kinds of Cajun spices, cayenne pepper and red pepper and garlic salt and put it on racks in the wood burning stoves – just hot enough to dry it out."

In fact, it was on a day she was planning to turn a deer into venison jerky that Ingrid's sister, Dee, made a surprise visit, bringing her daughter, Darla, with her.

"We had just shot the deer and quartered it and had it laid out on the table ready to cut up for jerky," recalls Ingrid. "Dee took one look at the deer, shielded Darla's eyes, and said, 'Oh my God, how could you do this to me?'"

"How could I do it to *her?* She was the one who came unannounced!"

What Ingrid found particularly amusing was that later on when they were sitting around the dinner table, Dee tasted a slice of venison jerky and said, "Ummm, this is good."

"City" squeamishness such as Dee had shown in response to the deer was not allowed among the Reeves children. "Richard and I insisted that the children had to help kill the rabbits and chickens and dress the deer. We warned them not to get friendly with the rabbits because we were raising them to eat for dinner."

With nearly every waking moment on the mountain a

teaching or learning moment for both children and adults, Ingrid grabbed the opportunity for a teaching moment when Thanksgiving approached one year.

"I thought we'd show the children that you don't just buy a turkey at the supermarket and bring it home for Thanksgiving dinner. We raised two turkeys from little babies. They waited and waited to kill those turkeys for Thanksgiving, and then it turned into a fiasco!"

All the children had a chore to do when turkey-killing day arrived. Heidi was to keep the water boiling and pluck turkey feathers. Wayne, Jason and Chris were stationed at a big tree stump with an axe. Jason and Chris were to hold the turkey down while Wayne swung the hatchet and cut off the gobbler's head. Unfortunately, Wayne's swing was not completely on target and the nearly headless turkey escaped, running helter-skelter and squirting blood all over the place. Chaos ensued as the turkey was chased down, finally captured and cut and thrown into the boiling water for plucking by Heidi. All dressed out, the very-well-fed Reeves Thanksgiving turkey weighed twenty-eight pounds. Ingrid literally had to shove it into the wood-burning oven to make it fit.

The other turkey later met with a quieter demise and was stored in pieces in the small freezer of one of the propane refrigerators.

Ingrid's favorite meat was, and still is, rabbit. "We didn't do much pork back then, and don't do it at all nowadays," she says. "As far back as I can remember I always cut the fat off of everything. I didn't use the skin of the chicken when I would grind up chicken and turkey for burritos. Once in a while we'd have beef, but our mainstay was rabbit. Rabbit meat is awesome. Chickens will eat anything, but a rabbit only eats nice veggies."

Raising their own rabbits for meat, Ingrid nearly always had rabbit on hand for her delicious chili and rabbit curry. She used the unique East Indian spices, onions, lots of garlic, ginger, tamarack, broccoli, cauliflower, red and green peppers, carrots, tomatoes, and a combination of wild and white rice.

"I practically raised the kids on curry," she says, "and everyone liked my burritos, in spite of the fact that I ground up all kinds of veggies in them."

Determined to provide as healthy a diet as possible while living mainly off the land, Ingrid and Richard tried growing vegetables in their little mountain valley, but were unsuccessful. The animals would get to them before the humans could. The only vegetables that they managed to grow were rutabagas and cherry tomatoes, neither of which apparently appealed to the animals. Neither of them were too popular with the humans, either, although when Ingrid announced that the kids could eat all the cherry tomatoes they wanted, both Wayne and Heidi developed a cherry tomato rash from eating too many at one time.

One thing Ingrid insisted on was that the family sit down together to eat breakfast and dinner, either sitting around the fire pit or at a dining table, but lunch was a meal that she usually prepared right along with breakfast.

"I'd pack good lunches for all of us every day," she recalls. "Jason, especially, was so skinny that I added extra soft-bake Toll House cookies to his lunches."

Ingrid made peanut butter and jelly sandwiches, tuna fish and egg salad sandwiches, turkey hotdogs and Vienna

sausages, and, of course, venison jerky. They'd have carrot and celery sticks, oranges and tangerines, and sometimes they'd have left-over cold fried rabbit. There was always a thermos of milk or juice. "The men at work were always trying to buy Richard's lunch from him."

Once a week, usually on a weekend day, Ingrid would get up at the crack of dawn, even earlier than 5 a.m., and wash all the family clothes by hand.

"I had an old wringer washing machine," she recalls. "I washed everything and then hung it all out on an old fashioned spinning line with clothespins. Richard will not wear anything that's not ironed – to this day – and I had four of those old-fashioned irons that I heated on top of the stove. I washed and ironed all day long."

The kids wore Levis three days in a row, but had enough socks and shorts and t-shirts to last for a week or more. Jason and Heidi, she remembers, were very hard on shoes, and went through them quickly. "We'd go to Van's Sneakers, and one whole paycheck would go for shoes for the four kids."

At meals, each of the kids had a designated sitting spot and a designated cup with their name on it. "They always made fun of me for that, but we didn't have enough water to do a lot of dishes and they had to keep their own cups clean, for brushing their teeth and for meals, too."

Now that Heidi is a mother, she has told Ingrid she understands about the designated cups and thinks they are a good idea. Having designated cups probably helped keep the kids healthier, as they were less likely to share their germs.

As for the formality of having their designated spots at meals, Ingrid and Richard wanted the children to know they

were each important and integral to the family structure.

"We said grace at special occasions and we were always very thankful for our food, but we did not raise the kids with any sort of religion except the religion of good character, compassion, honesty and respect," says Ingrid. "I wanted them to have respect for their elders. There was always room at our table or campfire for others and they were taught to be mannerly and give up their chair or their place if an elder needed one. Whenever we took them to a restaurant, the waitress would always comment, saying 'your children have the best manners.' They did have good manners and they had excellent self-discipline, too."

Richard was a tough taskmaster in several respects, not the least of those being education.

"Always, always, they had to do math and reading," recalls Ingrid. "Even in the summer, they had to do math for an hour during the day, and Richard quizzed them on it. They had to read, and we told them we'd let them buy any book they wanted, as long as they read it through."

The entire family enjoyed playing board games such as chess, scrabble, and Risk. "I never learned to play chess, but they all played," recalls Ingrid. "The game I loved was Risk and it got to the point that the kids started trying to get out of playing. I devised a plan to keep them in the game – the one who quit or lost first had to do the dishes!"

On many nights they gathered around the fire pit and sang songs and listened to the music of the mountain – the wind and the animals, the birds and the rustle of the sugar bush trees. Ingrid remembers those nights with great nostalgia. Even today, she stops to listen to the music and remembers the faces and voices of those little ones she nurtured in a circle of love on the mountain.

On May 8, 1979, Ingrid wrote a passionate love poem to her husband and her valley. Writing much like she talks … in simple, but sparkling vignettes of delightful observation, Ingrid's voice can be heard in the words of her poetry, and her heart shouts love and warmth in every line. Living in their valley on Reeves' Mountain was a daily adventure with her man and children. Life was good and Ingrid was inspired to express her joy in a poem titled "Our Valley."

Our Valley is filled with warmth and love,
With birds singing music from the break of day,
Then the wise old owl is here to stay.
He whoots and he whoots in the middle of the night
Oh my gosh!
I smell a smell that says run for your life!
A skunk is moving her family,
She thinks she is doing things that are right.

Our Valley is filled with warmth and love,
With animals of many shapes and sizes
Sent here from above
Quails, Bobcats and Snakes,
With twigs and leaves you clean up with a rake.
Many furry rabbits running here …
And, once in a while, a herd of brown-eyed deer.

Our Valley is filled with warmth and love,
With flowers all around us,

Colors like an artist's palette,
Spread over the hills and through the valleys.
The brush of brown and green
Make the boulders take forms of many different things
a man's eyes have never seen.
Our Valley we love and just change here and there,
But make it seem untouched by people living here.
Our Valley, to us, is warm and true,
Our Valley, in us, We will never leave you.

By Ingrid Reeves, May 8, 1979
Written for my husband who inspires me so very much!

Living so far out from the rest of society, the Reeves family bonded like few modern families bond. In fact, they actually originated their own tribal name (the Fagawees) in the course of their weekly hikes up the mountain. The hikes were led by Richard, the great white hunter, with his gun at the ready in case they ran into dinner along the way.

They proceeded in a line: Richard was followed by Ingrid, Wayne, Jason, Heidi and Chris – always in that order. Motioning for the Peter and the Wolf-like marching procession to come to a halt, his feet firmly planted on a mountain bluff, Richard would shade his eyes, peer off into the distance and utter the classic query: "Where the Fagawee?"

Thus, the *Fagawee* tribe was born.

"We are still the *Fagawees* to this day!" declares Ingrid, grinning at the memory. "And Richard still thinks it's a funny thing to say when we take guests out to see the property."

Heidi remembers the rigidly regimented family hikes

fondly. “Richard was always in the lead and Chris always brought up the rear. We’d be walking along and all of a sudden – Boom! Boom! Richard had shot something for dinner – rabbit, or rattler, or quail.”

“We don’t like to kill anything unless it’s going to be eaten,” Ingrid said, remembering the time that Wayne had to eat a tree squirrel.

“He killed it – he ate it. We never believed in killing just for the sake of killing.”

Rattlesnakes were the exception. There were rattlers everywhere when they moved to the mountain and began clearing land.

“We were afraid they’d kill the kids or the animals,” says Ingrid. “We’d kill them and feed them to the cats, so they didn’t go to waste.”

Rattlesnake heads had to be cut off and buried so that the dogs couldn’t get at them because their venom was still deadly even after death. There were usually two or three ranch dogs running around and several cats as well. Richard and Ingrid were in sync as to their love of animals and Richard was known for showing up with a new animal to join the already diverse menagerie.

A hardy pioneer woman who is not afraid of anything, especially hard work, Ingrid reveled in the life that she and Richard had chosen for themselves and their children.

From the time they first began dating and spent most of their dates on camping trips with the kids, Richard and Ingrid seemed to be preparing for the challenging life they would eventually live on the mountain.

There was one particular trip to Washington state

that the whole family remembers vividly. They camped at Willimac State Park.

"This night," Richard announced dramatically, "We're going to survive with nothing that we've bought from the store. We're each going to forage for our dinner."

Ingrid remembers there was just a little water at Gig Harbor that night when the tide went out and there was a huge halibut flopping around in the shallows. Richard threw a buck knife at the halibut and pinned it perfectly. "He's good with a knife," she notes.

That was also the night Ingrid learned to recognize a huckleberry. Jason, age 7, picked some berries and when she asked if they were edible, he responded, "You big dummy! Those are huckleberries and if the squirrels can eat them, you can eat them!"

After that, the kids went out huckleberry hunting and came back with pans full of raspberries, too. Jason also knew, from Boy Scouts, that pine needles made good tea. So, they had pine needle tea, huckleberries, raspberries and halibut for dinner that night. The kids also found some clams, and those were added to the menu. It was a deliciously wild "found" dinner, and it proved to all of them that they could survive quite well in the wilderness. That camping trip to Washington provided a lesson well-learned. They were all destined to learn many more survival techniques during the next dozen years.

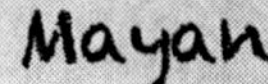

legend says the first two hummingbirds were created from the small feather scraps left over from the construction of other birds. The god who made the little birds was so pleased with his creation that he had an elaborate wedding ceremony for them. First, butterflies marked out a room, then flower petals fell on the ground to make a carpet; spiders spun webs to make a bridal pathway, then the sun sent down rays which caused the tiny groom to glow with dazzling reds and greens. The wedding guests noticed that whenever he turned away from the sun, he became drab again like the original gray feathers from which he was made.

Chapter 6

The Living With Richard Show

"We were green before it was fashionable," jokes Ingrid, remembering the many innovative methods that Richard rigged up to help the family survive on the mountain without electricity.

"In fact, now when Richard and I watch that show, 'Living with Ed,' we just laugh. Richard did those same things and more thirty-three years ago!"

For those who are unfamiliar with the "Living with Ed" Show, it is a popular California television series that combines comedy with serious environmentally friendly tips for sustainable "green" living. The show features actor and environmentalist Ed Begley, Jr. and his not-so-green Valley girl wife, actress Rachelle Carson. Their weekly adventures involve solar energy, recycling, living off the grid, and the many challenges they encounter as they try to maintain a healthy, simple lifestyle in the middle of suburbia.

One episode of "Living with Ed," featured Ed Begley, Jr., attaching a bicycle to a battery charger so that the energy of pedaling would generate enough electricity to turn on the toaster so that Ed could have his toast for breakfast.

That episode was particularly amusing in that the "Living with Richard" show featured that exact same bicycle and battery charger trick three decades ago, only there were four children taking turns pedaling like mad in order to watch an hour of television or turn on an electric lamp for late night homework or reading.

While the "Living with Ed" show is a fairly recent attraction and had run about three seasons at this writing, the "Living with Richard" show had a twelve year run, and featured a diverse and exciting cast of characters that included not only the legendary "Fagawee" tribe, but nearly every manner of mountain wildlife from skunks to rattlers to tarantulas and more.

The original untelevised Triple R Ranch "Living with Richard" show, particularly during the early years when the kids were in grade school, had daily episodes that would certainly have kept audiences glued to their televisions.

Episode One: "The Rattler that wouldn't die!"

When a young friend of Jason's witnessed the killing of a very large rattlesnake, she asked if it was good to eat.

"Mom," Jason asked, "Will you cook it for us?"

The rattlesnake was the biggest one they had ever seen. It was at least six feet long and as big around as a human arm, with eighteen rattles on it, which meant it was probably around eighteen years old, as a new rattle (or button) appears with each molting. The boys cut off the head, the rattles, skinned it, gutted it and brought Ingrid a huge coiled pile of beautiful white meat. She put it in a pan of water with salt on the hot stove to let it soak. Suddenly, Ingrid sensed movement.

"The thing curled up and began striking at me!" Ingrid remembers, shuddering. "No head. No tail. It jumped out of the pan onto the floor. The meat was slithering around my feet trying to strike at me!"

Intrepid Ingrid reached down, grabbed the writhing meat and threw it back in the pan.

"There's no way I'll eat this thing!" she yelled to anyone in hearing distance as she chopped it up in little pieces, breaded it like chicken and fried it for dinner.

Episode Two: "The Night Before Christmas"

Heidi remembers a Christmas Eve when the "pickin's were slim, and the hopes even slimmer." She and her brothers went to sleep knowing that their mountain was much too remote for a visit from Santa. Besides, Richard and Ingrid had warned the kids there would be no Christmas presents this year because there was no money.

"We kids spent most of the night feeling sorry for ourselves," Heidi remembers. When Christmas morning dawned, Ingrid and Richard directed the children to look out in front of the trailer and there, in the dirt, was a fleet of shiny yellow Tonka™ Trucks.

"Wow! Nice!" yelled the three boys, racing toward the trucks. Heidi stood stock still.

"What's wrong, Heidi? You don't like tractors?" asked Richard, sincerely perplexed. Upon seeing the expression on the little girl's face, he knew that something had to be done.

"Ingrid, you'll take Heidi to town today to buy her a

doll, or something," he stated, causing Heidi to perk up quite a bit. "It is a nice memory I have of Richard," recalls Heidi today, remembering the excitement that she felt as a little girl going to town with her mother to buy a special gift of her own choice.

"We agreed on a new doll at the store. We brought her home and took her out of the new box. I was made to feel very special on that Christmas day, being the only girl. It is a memory that I cherish still."

Episode Three: "The Great Frog Race"

The first spring rain, usually around March or April when Spring Break was underway, signaled that it was nearly time for The Great Frog Race to be held. A Reeves family tradition, The Great Frog Race originated when the kids began playing with the dozens of little frogs that suddenly appeared in the puddles and ponds of their mountain valley after a rainfall. The tiny two-inch frogs were either brown or green depending on their perch. When the land dried up again, they would disappear as quickly as they appeared.

Research reveals that these were probably indigenous Baja Tree Frogs (a misnomer, as they are rarely found in trees, but prefer earth and water habitats). In the dry, rainless summer months, the frogs hibernate.

So, it was on a weekend in late March following a couple of days of steady rain, with the pond full and the puddles jumping with frogs, that Richard announced, "Let the Great Frog Race begin!"

The rules were simple. Each child was required to build his or her own racing boat and make it big enough to hold one frog. The boats were made from cardboard or balsa wood (actually, the balsa wood was dried yucca stalk), with colorful construction paper sails. Using scissors, glue and pocket knives, toothpicks, tape and ingenuity, each of the young competitors fashioned a floating frog frigate that was guaranteed to sail straight to victory!

"My boat's faster than your boat!" "Oh yeah, well mine's bigger and when you put a frog in it, yours will sink!" "Well, my boat is the prettiest ... look, I painted the sail green and gold to match my frog!" "My boat has a secret ingredient this year that will guarantee a win!"

Wayne, Chris, Heidi and Jason sat amid a pile of scraps, putting the finishing touches on their boats, and vying for verbal victory before the race even began.

Pocketing their frogs, boats in hand, they headed down to the pond, following Richard, the Race Master, and Ingrid, the Timer.

"Ready, get set, GO!" shouted Ingrid, as the frog-bearing boats were launched toward the far bank with hearty pushes from their respective captains. And then, cheering from the sidelines all the way, the children ran to the opposite bank and crouched there, each urging their own boat toward the finish line. All but one, that is. Jason's boat appeared to be turning around and heading the other way.

Grinning a secret grin, ten-year-old Jason crouched down and began fumbling with something he held in his hand.

Soon, Jason's frog, with the boat close behind, was literally flying past the other boats. Jason had tied fishing line to the frog's leg and tied the frog to the boat. Ingenuity won the day, and the $5 grand prize! It was a Great Frog Race that became a family legend.

Episode Four: "Buried Treasure"

Once again, it was Spring Break, and all four kids were at the Triple R Ranch. Wayne and Jason were really getting fed up with Heidi and Chris. Not only did their younger siblings have no respect for the concentration their older brothers needed to play Dungeons & Dragons™, but they had actually made up their own language, complete with alphabet. It was an irritatingly unintelligible language that only the two of them understood. Constantly underfoot, conversing endlessly in their own ridiculous language, interrupting important D&D encounters, and just generally being pests, Heidi and Chris were about to be taught a lesson.

"We were tired of them nosing into our gaming and stuff. They were driving us crazy, so we devised a plan that would keep them away," recalls Wayne.

The plan took quite a bit of detailed preparation. Whispering just loudly enough to be overheard, Wayne and Jason talked about the treasure they had buried in a secret location ... so secret that they had created a treasure map to lead them back there. They talked of how they'd hidden the treasure map where Chris and Heidi would never find it.

"Little ears" eavesdropped eagerly. Several hours of peaceful "alone time" ensued as the younger siblings searched diligently for the hidden treasure map. Once found, the elaborate map led them on a merry chase in several directions, even directing them to Part 2 – a second treasure map – and finally to the obvious "secret" burial location.*

"We had to make it obvious," jokes Wayne. "They weren't the brightest kids on the block. Not only did we pace it out, but we put footprints in the sand and a bunch of rocks in the shape of a big X where we had buried the treasure, so they couldn't miss it."

Watching Heidi and Chris dig furiously, Wayne and Jason could barely contain their laughter. To the dismay of the treasure hunters, the buried treasure was a shoe box filled with a substance that was ordinarily buried in a blue bag in a remote place on the property. "They left us alone after that," notes Wayne.

*"Little Ears" reminds Ingrid of a classic Heidi story. Richard was talking privately with Ingrid and when Heidi repeated something he said, Richard commented, "She's all ears!" Heidi burst into tears upon hearing that remark. "I have a body!" she wailed. "I do, too, have a body!"

Episode Five: "Diving for Dollars"

"It gets horrifically hot out here in the summer – 115 degrees sometimes. The chickens and rabbits were dropping

dead in their cages. We'd put wet burlap bags over the cages to cool them down, but we still lost some," recalls Ingrid.

Every day in the summer when the kids were out of school, Ingrid would take them to Lake Perris. Richard would meet them there after work. There were twelve beaches at Lake Perris – numbered one through twelve – about two miles in all.

"We'd line up with the kids at Beach One, each of us with our fins, snorkel and a little goodie bag. Then we'd begin snorkeling about eight feet out – the youngest ones closer to shore – right next to where people were standing waist deep in water. Money was magnified down there. We found all kinds of jewelry, too. Finders-keepers – it was the Mariner's Law – and there were so many people who drank too much and fell in with their clothes on, or lost change from holes in their pockets. Sometimes, by the time we got to Beach Twelve, we'd have as much as $50 – enough to take the kids to the dollar show at the air-conditioned theater and buy popcorn, too!"

The kids got to keep whatever coins and treasures they found ... it was considered an allowance of sorts. The Lake Perris expeditions were a perfect way for the Reeves family to cool off and come away with some cool cash! Once, Richard even found a crusted-over bracelet that, when cleaned, turned out to be a very old and beautiful silver hand-carved Indian bracelet. Ingrid still wears it.

Sometimes, when they came up for air, people

swimming nearby would be stunned by the sudden appearance of this snorkeling family. Ingrid caught a big white goldfish (carp) in her hands one day and when she emerged, a lady swimming nearby said, "Tell me that's a fake fish." When she saw it squirm in Ingrid's hand, she ran screaming out of the water.

Little lobsters, "crawpappies" (or crawdaddies, depending on regional vernacular) were abundant on the bottom of Lake Perris, and the family would sometimes collect enough of them to have a delicious lobster boil back home on their mountain. Ah, the simple life!

Unfortunately, the idyllic days at Lake Perris were doomed. There was a day when Richard came out of the water feeling deathly ill. "I feel like I'm going to die," he said. Sure enough, the next day, there was an article in the newspaper about the lake being polluted. Eventually, according to Jason, it was nicknamed the "Perris Petri Dish" because it was a man-made lake with water pumped in by the water district, but no allowance for run-off.

Episode Six: "White Bread"

Richard brought home white bread! He nearly had a mutiny on his hands. Ingrid would never think of buying white bread, as she always insisted on whole wheat or multi-grain.

But this was a time when Richard was in charge of domestic things like grocery shopping and cooking – and these were definitely not in his repertoire. Ingrid, the heart of the home, was missing – and desperately missed! She had been injured at work and was undergoing surgery.

Ingrid remembers it this way:

"I worked at the Alumax Factory forming aluminum siding for mobile homes and it was backbreaking work – strenuous lifting and pushing all day long. My back had hurt almost continuously since Dee kicked me way back when I was a kid, but I'd kept right on with sports and dancing and heavy work – just ignoring the pain. There was one day at Alumax, though, when the pain went from bad to horrible! I couldn't walk. I couldn't even move. The pain shot from my big toe all the way up my right leg and into my back.

"The men were lifting me to get me to the company doctor and I kept shouting, 'No, no, no ... get a forklift ... don't try to lift me!' I weighed about 130 pounds and I thought I was so heavy!

"That was around 1980, before MRI's, and the doctors in Hemet couldn't find anything wrong with my back, but I knew this was serious. I went to the medical library and looked up Dr. Rhoue out at St. Bernardines in San Bernardino. He graduated from Loma Linda and was supposed to be the best surgeon around – he'd done back surgeries and brain surgeries. The doctor said I had degenerative disc disease, probably as a result of heavy lifting from the time I was five years old. My L-4 disc had totally shattered into my sciatic nerve.

"It required a three-hour operation to pick the shattered disc out of the nerve. The doctor told me I would have a drop foot from then on and that I'd end up in a wheelchair. I was determined not to have a drop foot or end up in a wheelchair, especially knowing that I needed to get back to taking care of the kids and Richard.

"If he would buy white bread at the grocery store, who

knew what other things they'd be eating. I had to get back on my feet fast!"

Episode Seven: "Hummingbird Heaven"

"The hummingbirds have always been here. They have always been part of my life and I didn't even realize it until now. They love the yellow trumpet trees that grow wild on our mountain. To the hummingbirds, they are just heavenly, even though some people treat the trees like weeds and cut them down. They are the mainstay for those beautiful little beings and we just pull the weeds out from around them and let the trumpet trees grow wild. I used to put hummingbird feeders out, with the sweet nectar they love, but the yellow trumpet trees and other plants that attract them are enough to keep them coming back year-round. Now that I've discovered how integral they are to my life, I'm learning that I was destined to identify with the hummingbird. Even the place of my birth – Trinidad – is known as 'The Land of the Hummingbird,' and there is a hummingbird on Trinidad's coat of arms and on the 1-cent coin, too! So, when the trumpet trees on our property are surrounded by hummingbirds, I know we are giving them a sweet taste of hummingbird heaven! It is all part of our Circle of Love!"

Episode Eight: "Granny's Delight!"

Heidi remembers a special destination in Sun City called Granny's Delight Ice Cream Parlor. "My mom would take us there about once a month and buy candy and ice cream. We put the candy in a big jar and were allowed to have one or two pieces a night."

One summer day when Ingrid took the kids to Granny's, there was a flyer on the counter advertising a contest, with a $25 prize going to the young artist who created the cutest picture of Granny's Delight Ice Cream Parlor. Twenty-five dollars! Ingrid had four young artists, all of whom were eager to win the prize!

"We sat around the dining room table with our paper, pens, pencils, and crayons," recalls Heidi. "It was intense. We were hiding our drawings from each other – everybody thought they had the winning idea. Mom turned all of our drawings in, and I won!"

Nine-year-old Heidi had drawn the big front picture window of the parlor with all of the different colored candies temptingly displayed. She had also drawn an airplane flying overhead with a banner that read "Granny's Delight Ice Cream Parlor." But in the spirit of fairness, Ingrid insisted that at least ten of the twenty-five dollars be spent on candy at the parlor.

*"I'm sure Mom took me shopping in town to buy something just for me," says Heidi, "but I remember just taking it for granted that I'd be sharing the $25 prize with my brothers. That's just the way we did things."**

* Speaking of the way they did things, Ingrid recalls with great

pride that the four children of their "merged marriage" were a truly cohesive team that accepted the need to share and also went out of their way to protect one another. When confronted with a "who dunnit" question from either Richard or Ingrid, sibling betrayal was never a factor. It became a family joke that everyone was always blameless because "The Ghost did it!"

Episode Nine: "The Meteorite that hit Chris!"

One dark night, they were sitting around the fire pit after eating dinner and cooking marshmallows. The embers of the fire were burning low and the night sky was bright with stars. Richard was ever the astronomy buff. He passed around his telescope and challenged the kids to count satellites, meteorites and shooting stars.

As so often happened with the Reeves family, it became a game: who could see the most meteorites – the first one to spot a meteorite or a meteorite shower would get the point. Chris was sitting on Richard's lap as his dad pointed out a large meteor shower. Fascinated, four-year-old Chris followed the meteor shower with his eyes. Suddenly, Richard yelled "Watch out! A meteorite is heading right toward us!"

Sure enough, something zoomed toward Chris, actually hitting him squarely on the chest. Chris screamed. Richard laughed. Soon, everyone was laughing. Richard had filled a bread bag with a couple of handfuls of dirt, tied it shut, and tossed it into the air directly above where he and Chris sat. The flight of the earthbound bread bag "meteorite" had been perfectly timed to coincide with the meteor shower happening in the sky. Forever afterwards, the story was told around the fire pit of the meteorite that fell to earth and hit Chris.

Episode Ten: "Have Tarantula, Will Travel"

Jason was fascinated by the wildlife that roamed the mountain, particularly the black California Tarantulas. "Tarantulas were harmless, and they made good pets," insists Jason. "Rosy boas were great, too. We learned very quickly which ones were good and which ones were bad. We had a bunch of encyclopedias and snake books and bug books and when we saw something we didn't recognize, we'd run look it up."

Jason and Chris spent a lot of time flying back and forth between the Triple R Ranch and San Francisco, where their mother lived, and there was one flight when Jason decided to take his pet tarantula home with him. "I had it in a coffee can. Chris and I took it to the ticket counter and told the man at the counter that I had a pet tarantula. He told me to tell the x-ray lady at security that there were a couple of cocoons in the coffee can for a school science project. When it went through the x-ray, the lady's face turned white and I told her, just like the man said, that it was a cocoon for a science project. She squealed, "That's not a cocoon. What is it!?"

The security guard opened the lid and slammed the top back on fast! The tarantula was probably the size of an orange – a typical black California Tarantula. The security guard looked long and hard at Jason and told him, "If that thing gets

out on the plane, you'll have a riot! You'd better keep the lid on tight." For some reason, Jason was allowed to board the plane with that coffee can, and the tarantula flew to San Francisco and ended up in the aquarium in Jason's room.

Episode Eleven: "Toothpick Birthday Gift"

It was Ingrid's birthday, January 24, 1979. Heidi, ten, and Wayne, twelve, stayed at home in charge of the Terry travel trailer while Richard took Ingrid out for dinner and a show.

"When we came home, they had gone to bed, but they had taken colored toothpicks and written, 'Happy Birthday Mom' on the rug. Heidi had blown out the inside of an egg and painted it real cute, put peanut shells on it for feet and toothpicks for arms and legs and a little hat made out of construction paper. The little peanut man was my present from her – sitting on the rug with the toothpicks around it. The children were always doing sweet, creative things and giving me little gifts that meant so much to me."

Ingrid constantly reminded the children that they didn't have to have money or spend money to give somebody something. "Go get some twigs," she'd tell them, "and make something with them. Gather some of these wonderful wildflowers and make a bouquet." The children, especially Heidi, would make beautiful birthday cards of their own design, with original verses in them. Ingrid still has some of those special mementos.

Episode Twelve: "There's Gold in Them Thar Hills!"

The Reeves' mountain is covered with huge boulders –

some of them as massive as homes – most of them made of rough granite. At the top of the hills are some white granite boulders that sparkle in the sun with golden glints of mica. When it rains, mica comes to the surface on the ground, too. The children would get so excited when they saw the mica, and they would spend hours panning for gold and come away with piles of mica pieces. "They thought it was gold when they were very young, and we warned them not to tell anybody, which made their discovery even more exciting," recalls Ingrid, with a grin.

"There are also beautiful red California garnets in the white granite. They look like gems ... and pink granite. Our mountain is filled with beauty and treasure. Richard and I have named most of the rocks on this mountain. We named one boulder Jaws because it looks like a great white shark. We named Elephant Rock because it looks like an elephant sitting there with big old floppy ears. Owl Rock looks just like an owl. There was a dinosaur cartoon show where there were dinosaurs and the baby would say, "Not the Mama! Not the Mama!" We named one boulder the "Not the Mama" rock because it looks just like that baby dinosaur.

Beanie and Cecil come from way back in the Fifties – they were puppets. One of them was a dinosaur head and wore a hat with a propeller. The Beanie and Cecil Rock looks like a whirly bird. Grandma Butt Rock looks like an old grandma with a wrinkled butt. The Indian Caves are boulders that are placed where you can crawl in and walk through them. There's a big boulder that looks like a squished flying dinosaur and another that looks like a Mammoth Footprint. Telescope (T-Rock) is the predominant rock way on the top of the mountain that looks like a telescope – it's our favorite. As you're coming home to Homeland – you see the T-Rock. Richard and I drive up there when I get home.

Episode Thirteen: "Bat Attack!"

True star-gazing required complete darkness. Often, the family would sit out on unpainted wooden chairs that they had bought from the gypsies and stare at the sky in silence for hours at a time. "It was pitch-black out there – you couldn't see your hand in front of your face," recalls Ingrid. "Jason, who wasn't afraid of anything and always had tarantulas and rosy boas for pets, was sitting in a chair one dark night while we all were trying to see who could count the most meteors, when a bat landed on his shoulder. It just sat there, and suddenly, he became hysterical. He was yelling "Get it off, get it off!" We were all just sitting there laughing at him. We'd never seen him afraid of anything before."

Episode Fourteen: "Fort Wayne"

Wayne was in 4th grade when they moved out to the mountain. One day while he was at school, Richard and Ingrid went to Home Depot and bought all the materials to build him a fort. Richard remembered having a neat fort built for him when he was a boy and he wanted to surprise Wayne with it when he got home.

"Fort Wayne" had a secret hatch door that could not be seen from the outside. The fort was about 8' x 8' and it was above ground on stilts – a sort of tree house minus the tree. You had to climb a ladder to get into it.

A boy who had earned the nickname of General Patton at school because of his all-consuming interest in all things Army, Wayne was absolutely thrilled with his very own fort. It instantly became his room and he slept in it from then on. One of the family dogs, Bandito, slept right underneath, acting as the General's sentry. It was a boy's dream come true.

While all four kids could fit in there, the fort was Wayne's domain. Many fierce army battles were waged from behind those protective walls. Many Dungeons and Dragons™ encounters occurred there, and it was his own special sanctuary when he wanted to be alone.

Even after he left home at eighteen and joined the infantry, Wayne would come back to the mountain on leave, squeeze into his old fort, stretch out to take a nap and dream boyhood dreams of army battles won and lost.

It was around 1987 when a wild fire swept through the property and destroyed several out buildings, including Wayne's fort. A man who had endured much pain and heart-break by age twenty, Wayne stood sadly at the site, wiped the tears from his face and squared his shoulders. Even with the hot ashes of his beloved fort scattered to the four winds, the resolve of "General Patton" remained strong. The heart remembers.

Episode Fifteen: "Cocktails Anyone?"

After her back surgery, Ingrid found she could not do the heavy lifting required by the factory, so she went to work as a cocktail waitress at night. "At first, I went to the junior college in Mount San Jacinto to be a medical assistant. I thought I'd like that type of work and I earned a certificate, *but when I was hired to work in the front office of a medical facility, I found out they wouldn't even pay me more than minimum wage, even after a year of earning a certificate!" Ingrid could have gotten a job typing, as she is a whiz on a manual typewriter to this day, but because they only had one vehicle and Richard needed to drive to Riverside, she got a job at the Winchester Inn, a little cowboy bar near Hemet, as a cocktail waitress. "I was making $100 a night in tips!" she declares. "Some of the girls who went to school with me wanted my job. The other waitresses working on weekends were registered nurses. I made more money there than I made at Alumax." This mother of four, in addition to washing all of their clothing on an old wringer washing machine, cooking on a wood-burning stove, cutting firewood, dynamiting boulders, and star-gazing in her spare time, also got a job as a hostess at the restaurant at Massacre Canyon, a golf course that was very popular with celebrities. She remembers the night that a very famous black boxer who was training there came into the dining room and Wayne happened to be there with her. After she introduced Wayne to him, the boy whispered a question to her. "Mama, if I rubbed against him, would I turn black like him?" Ingrid was stunned, but she knew it had nothing to do with prejudice. "Wayne simply wanted to be as good a fighter as the boxer was."*

Episode Sixteen: Pretty Spotted Skunks"

An animal lover who finds it difficult to shun any living creature, Ingrid was feeding the rabbits one day and felt one of the kittens rubbing up against her leg. She looked down and it wasn't a kitten. "It was a friendly little spotted skunk and I could see its family close by. There was no smell. It was so cute, I talked to Richard about getting them de-bagged, but he said no way, they carry rabies – get rid of those skunks! We got a tender trap and a very long pole. I sat in the back of our Ranchero and held the long pole with the tender trap and the spotted skunks in it and we took them to the wilderness about ten miles away. They were the only spotted skunks I ever saw – they were little and cute like kittens and I would have loved to keep them."

Kathryn Carter, Richard's mother, used to come out and live in a mobile home on the property part of the year. She loved all animals, too, and one day she found some newborn baby skunks that had been abandoned by their mother.

"She fed them by hand and they never sprayed her because they were content," says fellow animal lover, Ingrid. "They smelled, but not too horribly. They were tolerable."

Episode Seventeen: "Upright Bipeds"

There was a friendly neighbor woman who lived nearby when they first bought the property. Her kids would come and play sometimes with the Reeves bunch. Her friendly attitude changed abruptly a year or two later, though, around the same time that Ingrid's mother, Josephine, came for a visit. "She saw my mother and that's when the letters and law suits started coming," declares Ingrid. "She became the neighbor from hell, and to this day, I blame it on prejudice. She did not want a multi-ethnic family living next door."

Speaking of prejudice, and the phenomenon of being multi-ethnic – something that neither Wayne nor Heidi ever seemed to be confronted with – Ingrid was adamant that all of the children learn the importance of valuing all human beings for who they are rather than for what they are.

"When they began looking for jobs, I gave them this advice: On the part where it says race, write 'upright biped, planet earth, milky way galaxy, human being.'

"I've explained to the children repeatedly that we are all a melting pot. Wayne still calls me 'Mums' because my mom came from Trinidad. Everybody is everything – it depends on how far back you go - we have all evolved from the first beings and it's been said that those beings came out of Africa."

In episode after episode, the "Living with Richard" show was a witness to living life with gusto and imagination. Partnering in the great adventure series were "Richard the Green," the outdoorsman, hunter, inventor, astronomer and visionary, and the "Intrepid Ingrid," his beautiful, strong, creative and compassionate wife. Their four children – Wayne the Warrior, Jason the Innovator, Heidi the Helper and Chris the Charmer – each practiced their roles in the early years, playing them to perfection as the series followed them from toddler to teen and beyond.

Just as the family survived and thrived off the grid, the Triple R Ranch saga grew stronger and the music of the mountain sweeter with each passing year.

Tzunuum, the hummingbird, was created by the Great Spirit as a tiny, delicate bird with extraordinary flying ability. She was the only bird in the kingdom who could fly backwards and who could hover in one spot for several seconds. She was very plain; her feathers had no bright colors, yet she didn't mind. Tzunuum took pride in her flying skill and was happy with her life despite her looks.

When it came time to be married, Tzunuum found that she had neither a wedding gown nor a necklace. She was so sad that some of her best friends decided to create a wedding dress and jewelry as a surprise.

Ya, the vermilion-crowned flycatcher wore a gay crimson ring of feathers around his throat in those days. He decided to use it as his gift. So he tucked a few red plumes in his crown and gave the rest to the hummingbird for her necklace. Uchilchil, the bluebird, generously donated several blue feathers for her gown. The vain motmot, not to be outdone, offered more turquoise blue and emerald green. The cardinal, likewise, gave some red ones. Yuyum, the oriole, who was an excellent tailor as well as an engineer, sewed up all the plumage into an exquisite wedding gown for the little hummingbird. Ah-leum, the spider, crept up with a fragile web woven of shiny gossamer threads for her veil. She helped Mrs. Yuyum weave intricate designs into the dress. Canac, the honeybee, heard about the wedding and told all his friends who knew and liked the hummingbird. They brought much honey and nectar for the reception and hundreds of blossoms that were Tzunuum's favorites.

Then the Azar tree dropped a carpet of petals over the ground where the ceremony would take place. She offered to let Tzunuum and her groom spend their honeymoon in her branches. Pakal, the orange tree, put out sweet-smelling blossoms, as did Nicte, the plumeria vine. Haaz (the banana bush), Op (the custard apple tree) and Pichi and Put (the guava and papaya bushes) made certain that their fruits were ripe so the wedding guests would find delicious refreshments. And, finally, a large band of butterflies in all colors arrived to dance and flutter gaily around the hummingbird's wedding site.

When the wedding day arrived, Tzunuum was so surprised, happy and grateful that she could barely twitter her vows. The Great Spirit so admired her humble, honest soul that he sent word down with his messenger, Cozumel, the swallow, that the hummingbird could wear her wedding gown for the rest of her life. And, to this day, she has.

Chapter 7

Pink Hard Hat

Until around 1984, when Richard's employer, E. C. deYoung, advised him that they were closing their business, the famous "Fagawees" of the Triple R Ranch lived frugally, but well, surviving off the grid and never lacking for food, clothing or shelter.

That business closure proved to be the catalyst for Richard and Ingrid to take their next unique leap of faith – this time into the entrepreneurial world of business ownership. Once that leap was taken, their journey to the top of the mountain was truly underway.

With thc kind consideration of a heads-up from their boss about the planned closure, Richard and long-time business associate Dennis Woodland were able to begin pursuing a dream they had discussed, but had not believed would ever become reality. They began making preparations to go into business together.

The two men and their very supportive wives, Ingrid

and Vicky, visited an attorney and drew up a business plan. The business, in fact, was established as a woman-owned business, with Ingrid the major stockholder. The attorney looked at Richard and said, "Are you sure you know what you're doing?" and Richard said he was sure. It would be the beginning of a very lucrative partnership between the Reeves and the Woodlands.

Dennis had been in charge of building the parts that Richard, the structural engineer, had designed. Reading the blueprints and telling others how to build things, Richard and Dennis both came away from work each day with a lot of ideas on how things should be done and what the power plants needed. So even before the company closed down, Dennis had set up his own little shop called Woodland Welding and Richard had begun to work on earning his Class-A Engineering Contracting License.

As always, Richard's acquisition of the necessary next-step for advancement was a joint enterprise shared by his devoted helpmate, Ingrid, the majority stockholder and the "Jill of all trades" who was destined to wear her pink hardhat with great authority.

Studying the voluminous Class-A Engineering Contracting books at night after a full day's work would have been nearly impossible for Richard. He would have had to squint at the small print in the dim light of kerosene lanterns, and the studies might have dragged on for years rather than the short months they had in mind. So, Ingrid read the books out loud by day into a small battery-operated recorder, producing little cassette tapes that Richard could listen to in the car on the way to work.

"Both of us were learning!" declares Ingrid, adding that even with that efficient method perfected, the studies lasted for six months.

Finally, Richard felt ready to take the test for licensure. On the appointed day, Ingrid went with him to Riverside and sat in the car waiting while he took the test. It was an all-day ordeal, lasting from 9 a.m. to 6 p.m., so Richard took his lunch in with him. But Ingrid remembers that about halfway through the test, a bunch of people came streaming out of the building.

"I waited and waited, and finally, at 6 p.m., Richard walked out," recalls Ingrid. "I asked him why those other people left so early and he said the test was way too hard and a lot of people just gave up and walked out."

Then the waiting began in earnest, as it took about three days before notice arrived in the mail that Richard had earned his Class-A Engineering Contracting License. He had been told that it generally took two or three tries to pass the test, but with the competent help of his wife, and his innate intelligence and experience, Richard had come through with flying colors the first time.

"He's so smart. There's just about nothing he can't do," says Ingrid. "And, with that Class-A Engineering Contracting License, he could have done just about anything he wanted. He could have built freeways, dams, bridges, whatever, but we just chose to work in power generation plants because that's what he and Dennis knew, and because we wanted to stay small – a family business. We had seen too many big businesses out there that have bad habits of buying people and bribing customers, which is something we've never done. To us, that's not the way to get a job. We had to compete with a

lot of those big companies, but it didn't take long for the industry to recognize our good work. We incorporated in 1986 and since then, Richard has become the guru of air pre-heater overhaul, and now, with Richard beginning to slow down, Jason is the Junior Guru."

Today, when Ingrid jumps down from the *Reeves & Woodland Industries* truck and dons her pink hardhat at the worksite, it's serious business. From the time she was five, when her mother put a bucket and brush in her little hands and ordered her to scrub floors, Ingrid has taken work very seriously, indeed, and that work ethic has not changed one iota.

"You can send people to dot the i's and cross the t's, but there's no one in the world like Ingrid," says Richard. "She's signed every contract we've ever entered. Wherever she was needed, she's been there. She's even helped make steel grids! Ingrid has been the backbone of this company."

The first bid made by Reeves & Woodland Contractors was for a job at San Diego Gas & Electric Company, and they won the bid.

"We celebrated and then we went to work," recalls Ingrid. "That's what we did then and that's what we've always done. It has been a great partnership between Dennis and Richard, too, because both of them are workaholics. They even look like brothers. Dennis's wife, Vicki, has always been supportive, but she's never jumped into the middle of the business like I did."

Dennis Woodland was seventy-one years old in 2011 and had undergone a quadruple bypass, but he still worked daily in his Woodland Welding Shop in Perris, while Richard, who was almost old enough for Social Security, continued to run Reeves & Woodland and RR Contractors – the other two connected companies owned by Richard and Ingrid.

On the Reeves & Woodland Industries, Inc. website (www.reevesandwoodlandind.com), the impressive introduction states:

"Reeves & Woodland Industries is a California based manufacturing and field service company founded in 1986 by Richard Reeves and Dennis Woodland. Since then, Reeves & Woodland has been continually designing, manufacturing and installing high efficiency sealing systems for rotary type, regenerative air preheaters. Our technical staff has over 50 years experience overhauling, refurbishing and custom designing sealing systems for air heaters. This experience has helped us become a leading air heater supplier of sealing components on the West

Coast. Thanks to our reputation for results, our attention to details and technical expertise, R & W sealing components are in nearly all fossil fuel generation plants in California, as well as numerous other installations around the country and the world."

The company profile reads:

"Reeves & Woodland Industries currently has three manufacturing facilities in California and our company prides itself on a quick response time. Our facilities can usually cut the lead time for parts by more than half of what it takes our competitors. In emergency shutdown situations, we are often the only company that can have parts on the station in days, not weeks. With our technical representatives in the field, working in direct contact with our manufacturing facilities, we can custom make air preheater components that guarantee a proper fit thereby reducing leakage.

Reeves & Woodland offers a large selection of seals, structural components and services. We have performed considerable research and development of replacement air preheater products and installation procedures and are continuously working towards further developments. Reeves & Woodland has been highly successful in the area of tight sealing heaters through the use of our patented <u>High Efficiency Flexible Contact seals</u> and controlled installation procedures."

The company's patented *High Efficiency Flexible Contact Seals* are among Richard's most innovative inventions.

In describing exactly what it is that the company does with sealing air preheaters, Richard puts it this way: "If you think of it like a car radiator – a lot of heat comes out of the engine and the radiator cools off the heat. The air preheater captures the heat and recycles it through a large rotating mass of steel and promotes fuel efficiency. Instead of using thousands of gallons of gas, the air preheater tunnels and recycles the heat."

"We invented a better way of sealing the air preheater in electrical power plants so that you can capture much more heat. It all goes back to efficiency. After working in the units for years at E. C. deYoung, we learned to always strive for the highest efficiency of any unit you're working on and we observed that rigid seals didn't remain tight enough during large heat exchanges and thermal turndowns – so we came up with flexible seals to comply with the irregular turndown. The flexible seals are more efficient because they bend and mold themselves to the unit. With the tighter seal, there is less leakage and higher efficiency. Of course, we're always designing and redesigning the flexible seals in order to be even more efficient. A new unit often demands a new design."

Also, the flexing cycle of the seals takes place in extreme heat – sometimes four hundred degrees – and it is bent like a windshield wiper, back and forth, so the life of these seals is reduced compared to old rigid design. Because of the extra expense of replacing them more frequently, it took a while to convince these guys to spend the money to begin with, but they have discovered that it pays for itself after a few months, easily."

Although they specialize in tight sealing air pre-heater units, Reeves & Woodland inspects, rebuilds, refits, overhauls and replaces parts, providing general maintenance, usually in one to three year cycles, for many power plants throughout the state of California and beyond, working in several capacities – as contractor, manufacturer and inspector – and working on a personal basis one on one, year after year.

"There are three different levels to our business," explains Richard. "We go in and inspect, writing a report with recommendations about part replacement, then we put in a bid for the power plant to buy our own manufactured parts, and then we send in our people to do the work."

According to Richard, the air heaters weigh between a half a million and three million pounds. "It's like a big Ferris wheel – plumb full of metal – or a giant carousel. We also make the corrugated metal and each of these units has different corrugation designs. It's a tough, dirty job and it is massive. On some jobs, we're flying with cranes up in the air to do the work. It's very dangerous and takes excellent coordination. Everyone wears hard hats and safety glasses, and there is incredible heat. They shut down the unit and cool it off before we work on it, but it is still hot."

The environment in which they work at the power plants is extreme in every way – extreme temperatures, extreme pressures, and extreme danger. There is a mandatory thirty-minute safety meeting each morning at each power plant for the Reeves & Woodland staff.

Ingrid, who accompanies Richard on nearly every job, is very proud of the fact that Reeves & Woodland has won safety awards many times over the years, despite the daunting size and resources of their huge, many-layered, international competitors.

"We're like a little bumblebee when compared to our big competitors," jokes Richard. "But, once in a while, we sting them."

Due to the huge demand for electricity during the summer months, Reeves & Woodland does their overhauling and maintenance work during the winter months only.

"When they're shut down, they're not making any electricity, so the power plants schedule these overhauls carefully," said Richard. "We work for each plant on a specialty basis, trying to do everything we can and do a better job of detail and precision work than anyone else. Person to person – year after year – they usually come back to us time after time because of the level of work we do."

Talking of the strict OSHA Safety Rules and the many safety awards the company has won over the years, Richard explains that each area of work done by their contractors in the power plant is specified by the type of work and the necessity for compliance. For instance, if you are working up in the air, safety harnesses and safety belts are required. The atmosphere is tested continuously in the power plants as well.

"It can take half a day to do half a minute's work," notes Richard. "Jason and the field crew foreman that works for Jason meet with the prescribed safety organization that works for the power plant (safety managers that work with contractors), and this is the procedure every time you start a job."

In addition to signing every contract that the company has ever entered into, Ingrid acts as the office manager, providing support to the field crew.

"If we need something, she'll find it," said Richard. "She also used to attend all the safety meetings when she was working at my side in the power plants."

Ingrid recalls when she and Richard worked on the jet engine "Peakers" together. "Peakers run the generators that supply the peak energy to the air conditioners – they are the last of the last things to make electricity – they are the reserve and very expensive to run. They burn a bunch of fuel. We would do work on the Peakers in the middle of summer, but we don't do that much anymore," she says, remembering they would divide up into different chambers of the power plant, two people to a team – one person doing the welding and a helper to hand the welding rod.

"Richard and I would have one of the little compartments. He'd do the welding and I was his helper. We'd work circles around the other guys. We'd finish ours way before the rest of them. We were always a good team. I did everything from cut steel to arrange steel. The welders would come in and weld them up. Whatever

was needed, I would do. I'd drive the huge trucks with forty-foot trailers. I still drive those to the units today, but I'm getting away from it now. We serve all of California, and the drivers on the road are different today than they used to be."

For Ingrid, even after all these years, it is not easy to explain to people exactly what Reeves & Woodland Industries does. "We are divided into three companies – Dennis builds the parts in the shop, R.R. Contractors does the overhaul and puts it into the power plants, and Reeves & Woodland Industries does the rest. Richard is the genius behind it all. He's the one who saw what the units he was working on really needed and created the flexible seal for the air pre-heaters. Seeing what was needed and creating a solution for the need is something he's always done very well – from the time we bought the property until this very day."

"Our son, Jason, does all the computing stuff," says Ingrid. "It's all very technical now, but when we started this business, I was right there helping with the structural part of putting all the parts together, working on the steel-cutting saws, cutting the metal, lifting the metal – it was all family working together. Even Dennis used his boys for the shop. We used Wayne, Jason and then Chris. Heidi was never interested in the business – she wanted to be a school teacher. Heidi went to Hawaii after we started the business and just came home during the summer months. Heidi loved paper. She still does."

During those fledgling years of the company, all four of the children became teenagers and spent a good deal of time switching back and forth between their maternal and paternal families, Wayne going back and forth to Hawaii and Heidi

remaining there to graduate from high school. Jason and Chris had come to live with Ingrid and Richard by that time, but in his senior year, Chris went to live with his mother in the Redlands and went to school there. Jason stayed on the mountain.

"The teens went back and forth," recalls Ingrid. "We didn't argue with them, as long as they were with us either in the summer or winter."

Both Wayne and Jason went into the military right after high school graduation and that was something of which Richard and Ingrid highly approved.

Wayne graduated from Hemet High School in 1985 and was preparing, of course, to go into the Army as he had wanted to do all his life. But, prior to joining up, "General Patton" wanted to get "buff."

"He told me he was thinking of joining a gym. A gym! Can you believe it?" exclaims Ingrid. "I told him we had a mile of dirt road and a whole mountain of weeds where he could run up and down and bend and stretch to pick weeds to his heart's content. He could certainly get buff without joining a gym."

And buff he did get. Buff and ready for action, Wayne was in the 21st Infantry's Rapid Deployment Unit at Fort Stewart. He was the kind of soldier who never questioned authority and followed every order to the letter.

"One of the guys in my barracks was a real PTL (Praise the Lord) fan," recalls Wayne. "He preached constantly, especially to me. He kept telling me I was too violent and bloodthirsty; that I was too eager to kill somebody. He said I needed to pray to Jesus about it and be very sincere."

One night, just to satisfy his barracks buddy, Wayne prayed. "Jesus," he prayed, "if you don't want me to serve, then get me out of the Army."

The next morning, when his commanding officer ordered him up on a steep roof to retrieve a laundry bag that someone had thrown there, Wayne scrambled right up. The roof was steep and slanted and slippery, but gung-ho Wayne was determined to follow his superior's orders. As he reached for the laundry bag, he slipped and fell off the roof, landing three stories below, a broken man. He broke both arms and both legs, and, to this day, has screws in his legs and feet.

"When I hit the ground, I saw a big bright light with darkness behind it," recalls Wayne. "I heard a voice say, 'No! He's mine! He called upon me!' and the darkness disappeared. That's when I knew the Lord had me. I said, 'Oh, Jesus, please don't let me die in Georgia!'"

Geography aside, the Lord obviously had other plans for Wayne Street waiting back in California, and they did not include killing people. People who witnessed his fall from the roof confirmed that he never lost consciousness when he hit the ground, but remained coherent until well after he was transported to the hospital.

The next day when an Army chaplain visited his hospital room, Wayne told him the story of God's answer to his prayer, and his wide-awake experience with the bright light.

"I swear, that chaplain turned white as a ghost – and he was a black guy!" declares Wayne. "He walked out of the room and never came to visit me again."

Wayne laid there and pondered this strange reaction

from the chaplain. Instead of being thrilled at a true conversion event, the chaplain couldn't seem to handle it. "After that happened, nobody came with a Bible – it was just Jesus and me for a while. I had gone over the edge as far as violence is concerned, and I knew it now, and started going in a different direction," he says. "When I met my wife, Shirley, our ministry began."

Ingrid remembers the terror she felt when she heard about Wayne's accident. This was her first-born and she wanted to fly to him instantly and wrap him in her healing arms.

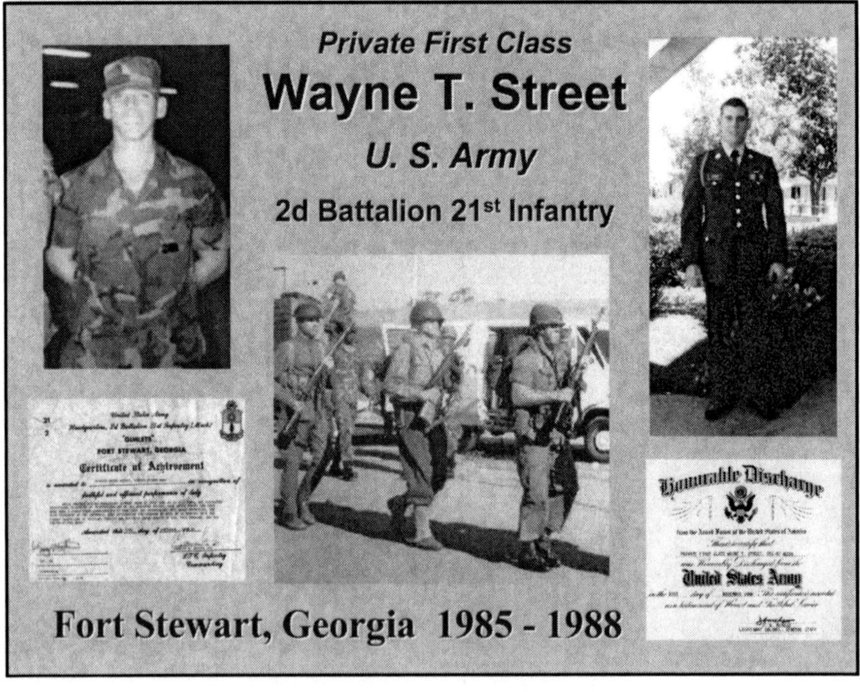

"They called us from Fort Stewart to tell us about Wayne," she remembers. "Richard and I grabbed the only vehicle we had and drove straight through to get to the hospital. We didn't have enough money back then to fly – in fact, we scraped together every spare cent we had just for the fuel. It was a terrible trip there and back, but Wayne was amazing. Instead of being bitter over losing his life's ambition and not being in the Army anymore, Wayne began writing Christian music."

Wayne had always been the one who accompanied Ingrid on his guitar when they sat around the fire pit and now, he turned to music and Jesus Christ for solace.

"He had never prayed before, to my knowledge, but he sure prayed then," recalls Ingrid. "He prayed to Jesus daily and asked Him what he should do. Richard wanted him to come to work with us, but structural steel was not the right kind of work for him."

Wayne did let Richard teach him how to weld and, according to his mother, he's a fantastic welder. It's an art to weld and he is an artist at it, but his heart is in playing his guitar and writing Christian music, and being outside, so he now combines his passions as a pool man and a missionary. Wayne and his wife, Shirley Jean, have a little band called Messengers of the Cross and they go into coffee shops and places and sing free of charge.

"Wayne is like me, though," says Ingrid. "No matter what happens, he'll never give up and he'll never give in. He hurts – he has screws and bolts in his feet – but he stands and cleans pools every day and he still surfs – he's an amazing man. I'm so proud of him."

Jason went into the Navy, following in his dad's footsteps, and was on the *U.S.S. Los Angeles*. He was a mechanic on the submarine and remembers that it was like a mini-power

plant. Now working with massive power plants, Jason is grateful for the training he received in the Navy and hopeful that his son, Jesse, now a machinist's mate aboard the *U.S.S. New Mexico* (another submarine), will emerge similarly prepared to go into the family business.

Chris worked for the company for a while after high school and became a highly respected technical representative before going out on his own. He now lives in Colorado and has his own company, occasionally contracting with Reeves & Woodland Industries as a consultant/technical representative with power plants in that area. Coincidentally (or maybe not), Chris has built a totally solar-powered home 10,000 feet up a mountain in Forbes, adjacent to an animal reserve. He and his family divide their time between that home and a century-old "painted lady" home in Pueblo, Colorado.

Heidi is married to a Navy helicopter mechanic named Joseph Conner and is the proud mother of three-year old Preston True Conner. "True" … Heidi is true to her love of paper and words, and now has the education to be a teacher, but prefers being a full-time mom and substitute teaching once in a while. She loves taking photographs and has taken some great ones of her brother, Wayne, and his band performing. Heidi lives nearby and sees Ingrid and Richard often. Whenever she can, Ingrid enjoys visiting with her beautiful Heidi Dawn and playing with that adorable grandson, Preston True.

As to the business being a family business, Jason is the one of the four children who has shown a strong interest in carrying on the business that is now nearly a quarter of a century old, and Jason's son, Jesse, is well on his way to following his dad's lead.

"It has become a good business," says Ingrid, remembering that it took about five years of incredibly hard work before the new business began showing a profit.

"We would sit there together after Richard did the spec – telling them what they needed at the power plant – and we would figure out the cost and put in our bid. It was a closed bid and there were many other companies much bigger than us bidding for the same job. We'd drive in the bid and then wait to find out if we won it. We wanted to be paid weekly. In fact, we had to be paid weekly because we didn't have the money and we would never borrow the money. It wasn't easy to get those bids asking them to pay us for the materials up front, but once we did get the bid and did the work, we usually had a customer for life."

Reflecting back on the days when she and Richard used to take the kids "diving for dollars" at Lake Perris, it is gratifying and somewhat unbelievable to Ingrid that they now own a company that makes million-dollar bids regularly.

And, although the trappings of wealth are enjoyed and never taken for granted, the hard working lady with the pink hard hat notes that there is something much more important to her than money.

"I've had money and I've been dirt poor," says Ingrid, "and the one constant through it all has been my concern for doing a good job and for taking care of the people in my life. It doesn't matter how much or how little I had, I always wanted to do whatever I did well and to make sure the people I loved were alright."

So, this year as in years past, when the Reeves & Woodland Industries, Inc. profit and loss statements came across her desk, Ingrid's first concern was not how many dollars there were to spend, but how many jobs were done well and safely, and how many mouths were fed.

"We had forty guys working for us last year, and that means forty families had food on the table," says Ingrid. "Even better than that, we had absolutely no safety issues or injuries last year. Every job was done and done right. Every single day I pray, please God and all the angels, help them do a good job and keep them safe on the roads, safe at work and safe at home. That is the ultimate profit for our company … food on the table and a job well done."

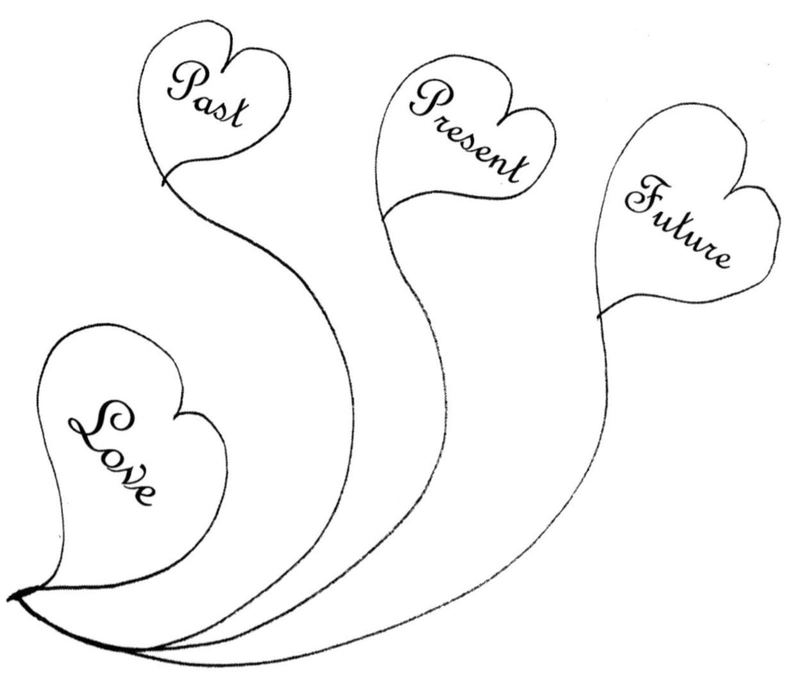

Heart of the Story … photos, poems, and more!

Ingrid's inner thoughts have often been expressed by poetry. In 1990, she was awarded a Golden Poet Certificate by the World of Poetry editor and publisher, John Campbell. Whenever the muse strikes her, Ingrid will sit down, put pen to paper, and compose a poem. Now that her many years of extreme work are beginning to become a thing of the past, Ingrid's poetic nature will have the chance to bloom and flourish.

Recently, Ingrid printed a little booklet of her poetry titled "Ingrid's Thoughts." Her Introduction delves deeply into her desire to reach out and provide healing to a hurting world, and her poems reflect her passion for life.

My thoughts to the human race, planet earth, Milky Way Galaxy, in the Carina Sagittarius Arm, planet earth so small …

"Do not judge a person by physical appearance or by color. Listen to their words, watch their actions, then you will hear the beat of their hearts, and know the notes to the music."
–Ingrid Yvette Reeves

Nationality

Hello my friend, my dear friend, what nationality are you? Well my friend, I'm multi-ethnic. I'll name all, so proud, so true. I'm Scottish, Irish, German, Jew. Many tears have been shed for being only these few. I'm French, Spanish, Carib Indian, British, too. Oh my friend, my dear friend, I hope I'm loved and judged for what I am within, and not by the color of my skin.

Confusion Everywhere on Freedom

Walls came tumbling down. Babies cried.

Born so free, Elders died. Told how to think, how to laugh, how to sigh, What may I say? What may I play? What of my belief? I see no relief. World all around, colors battle, hold your ground. Don't ask why. Is it mine? NO! It is OURS. Each one who breaths human breath. Do not devour. RED, YELLOW, BLACK, WHITE and BROWN. Red, color of a square, young minds slaughtered there. Yellow, myriad dead fellows. Black, ludicrous screams, charred, abused, set them in the back. White, so pure. Look closer now, a tinge of grey, traces of BROWN, YELLOW and BLACK, Brown, you are not from this town. CONFUSION EVERYWHERE ON FREEDOM.

Slow Down World
Mom, off to work,
Dad, off to work,
Children, off to school,
No time to care.

No time to give.
No time to talk.
No time to share.
No time to smile.
No time for me.
No time for you.
Material things, human greed,
Material things, how much do we need.
In life the body so warm.
In death so cold.
SLOW DOWN WORLD.

Oh Lord, I'm Just a Child

It's 2:00 a.m. A voice calls out, get up my child. It's time to clean and scrub the offices, our family must survive. Oh I want to sleep, I want to count sheep. Oh Lord I'm just a child. I open the door, what is before my eyes, a majestic ballroom. Mirrored sphere, suspended in the air, it whirls, twirls, luminous, color beaming. A handsome prince, may I have this dance. Violins, harpsichords, mandolins, flutes.

Door flies open, my mop drops with a clatter. CHILD! What is the matter, a voice screams with scorn – scrub, clean. There's an abundance more. Oh Lord I'm just a child. I look into the deep abyss. A leviathan? No, a radiant mermaid, frolicsome swims. Dolphins messmate wondrous things.

Door flies open, my bucket! Plunder, crash. CHILD! More

porcelain toilets, clean now flash. Oh Lord I'm just a child. I see the dawn, another night gone. No sleep. School, education. What's recreation? I'm expected to exceed. But how, I'm so very tired now.
OH LORD I'M JUST A CHILD.

STRONG ONE

You have moved into her life, so strong, so bold.
You have made her heartless, so cold.
You have taken her from reality, from hope, from dreams.
Nights, she shivers, quivers.
Strong one you have stolen another, my mother.
No love can she see.
Oh strong one, I hate thee.
She is so pale so frail,
A life tormented by a liquid fermented.
So irresistible, oh you're despicable.
She is so used from this bottle of booze

DECEMBER TREE

Mother earth holds my life.
An awesome figure in the night.
I soar into the atmosphere, most unaware.
Aromatic branches swaying, Children playing,
Feathered friends nestled within my arms.

Comfort I bring, for most everything.
It's the time of the season.
I'm cut with no reason.
Oh seize me with my earth abound.
I'm for exhibition, it's a tradition.
Luminous lights hung for delight.
Festive season is through.
I gave merriment to you.
Place me into the ground.
Mother earth abound.
My life is a need, so we all can breathe.

Ingrid points proudly to her son, Christian, as a writer of funny and imaginative prose. In a letter to Richard and Ingrid from Roanoke, Virginia in December of 1993, addressed to "Reeves Dork Farm," Chris, who avidly rides a mountain bike, included an original "insider science fiction sort of short story" entitled **"Adventures of the Bikemiester, #3 Boiling Bettys"**

"There's no trail too tough, no hill too steep, no danger too great, and as sure as you're drafting a rider with gas, THE BIKEMIESTER WILL BE THERE …" is the last line of his epic tale, and could be the premise for a real-life story about Christian's lifestyle.

Christian not only has a wild imagination and great command of the English language, but has formed some important insights into growing up on the Dork Farm.

In his 1993 letter, he asks his parents, *"So how are*

things on the California dork farm, Sunny probably! (add a jealous vehement snarl here). You know, it reminds me. I can remember all the times Dad would climb up on some rock somewhere (this is, of course, after the ritual "Fagawee" call), and proudly babble something about how it's sunny here and the rest of the country is under tons of snow. He would then pause for an instant, as if to be weighing the thought himself, before randomly finding some sort of insane job for me to do. However, I realize all too often now, how many of those incessant babblings were actually true, and unfortunately, they always surface from my subconscious as post-amenable realizations after the situation has already occurred. Kinda like finding myself locked in this godforsaken apartment while blizzard conditions persist outside, and you all are enjoying a sunny California Christmas.

Yup, I have to admit, I think of you often Dad and Ingrid, usually with a shake of my head and uttering under my breath, 'Didn't Dad tell me not to do that?' It's a scary realization, especially now that I'm going to have a child! (as if that wasn't scary enough in itself) because for the first time I realized I'm going to be doing the exact same things to my poor kid, all along trying desperately to shield him from the harsh realities of this world, knowing full well his perception of it is going to simply be, futile, senile, babblings. Is that the way it's supposed to be, with each generation doing the exact same stupid things as the one before it?"

Obviously, as Christian wrote about his impending fatherhood, he was thankfully reflecting on his upbringing, as he ended his letter thusly:

"I will say this before I go. I don't think I would have

all these memories and adventures and be the person I am today if it wasn't for the 'Dork Farm.' The more I think about it, the more I want to raise my dorks with the same Grade-A quality environment. So be sure to save 5 acres somewhere on that mountain, so they too can knock the shit out of their dad with Warriors, and spears, and WD-40, that I have no doubt their grandfather will supply.

Merry Christmas & A Happy New Year.

Love Always, Christian.

Heidi, too, looks back nostalgically on the days when she and Christian were running around on the mountain – two little "dorks" playing Liar's Poker and helping their mother make and eat the best chocolate chip cookies in the world.

Heidi looks forward eagerly to the day that her mother builds a mountain sanctuary because she wants to participate by teaching children to make her special fairy crafts. She enjoys the beautiful art of Josephine Wall, with its mystical, magical goddesses, mermaids and faeries, and is inspired by it.

"I love the make-believe world of faeries where one can escape reality now and then," says Heidi, who, like her mother, has a lovely way with words. Heidi wrote:

"Faeries talk both night and day. It's only that their voices are so small that we don't hear what they say."

Like her mother, Heidi also loves to quote Albert Einstein: *"Imagination is more important than knowledge."*

Imagination is in the aura that surrounds Ingrid. It spreads its wings across her mountain and valley in the stark beauty of the boulders strewn by the hand of God and lovingly named by the mind of man.

Our Favorite Boulders

(above) Harbor Seal Boulder

(above) Owl Boulder

(above) Leatherhead Boulder - like the old style football helmet

(above) "Jaws" Shark boulder with fish hanging out of his mouth; Mt. Baldy is in the background, covered with snow

(above) Beany from *Beany and Cecil*

These boulders are all on our property in California. Over the years we have named our favorites!

(left) Telescope Boulder

(above) The Thinker Boulder

(below) Pteradactyl Boulder

Indian Cave Boulder on right, with Solar System Boulder on left

Ingrid, Grand-niece Sheena,
sister Enid and brother Wally

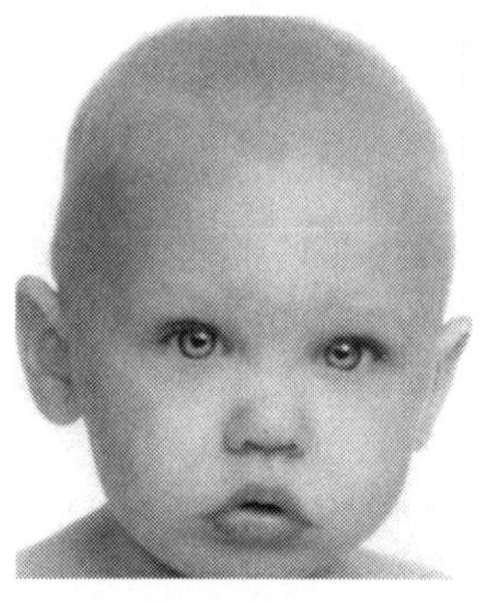

Preston True
at 1 year old

Heidi, Ingrid, and Wayne

Richard and Ingrid

Heidi Dawn Street

Ingrid and Granddaughter Beth Reeves on Jesse & Brittney's Wedding Day

Sister Davis Marcus 1954

Preston True on our mountain

Brother Frank Marcus

Daughter Heidi, Grandson Preston True, and Grandson Jesse Reeves on his Wedding Day Oct. 2010

Sister Enid and her son Kennith

Joseph Conner & his son Preston True

Heidi, Christian and Wayne, Azusa California

Ingrid, Grandson Preston True and Daughter Heidi

Josephine Marcus

Ingrid, her sister Enid & Enid's daughter Kim Kinores

Ingrid and Richard, 1974

Richard and Preston True

Sister Enid, Heidi & Preston True

Cousin Bernardo Marcus, Walter & Josephine Marcus

Frank Marcus, 1968

Sandy, Tara, Justin, Nathan, Sher with Pola, and Dana

Heidi and Wayne

Wayne Street

Walter & Josephine Marcus
with Ingrid

Ingrid with her Grandson
Jesse Reeves

Walter Sr. and Frank
with girlfriend Candy,
1966

Chapter 8

Love, Sunshine & Bubbles

Ingrid blows bubbles from the deck of their 42-foot trawler – hundreds of bubbles that float for a long time on the water, glittering in the California sunshine and in the smiling sapphire eyes of the bubble-blower.

"I love to blow bubbles," she says. "Deep in my soul, I've always felt this peaceful, happy inner spirit that seems to flow out with the bubbles, especially when they float so beautifully on the water."

The soft, lyrical words "love, sunshine and bubbles," signify the life that Ingrid and Richard have built for themselves through hard work and dogged persistence.

"We live well on our eighty-four acres of dirt, boulders and high desert," she says. "Every rock and boulder has a name. I see faces in everything – animals, birds, bubbles, boulders – it is still our sanctuary – more than ever – and I love it."

Today, when Ingrid blows bubbles from the deck of

their boat when it is anchored or calls dolphins to ride in its wake when it is underway, she enjoys the moment and savors the memories.

Those magical years of tracking the stars that sparkled in the black velvet of the night and trekking the mountain in search of edible prey by day are indelibly carried in the hearts of the family forever.

When Ingrid and Richard began buying their mountain, ten or twenty acres at a time, clearing the barren land of huge boulders, hauling in water, camping out with their children, they were virtually living the lives of early pioneers in the Southern California wilderness. Today, they live comfortably in what Ingrid refers to as a "stick home" (permanent, not mobile) with a twenty by forty foot swimming pool and spa, their old homestead completely renovated and improved with sheetrock and a clay tile roof.

Although they are now "on the electric grid," Richard has engineered their dwelling so that solar energy supplies quite a large percentage of their power, and so that they can survive quite well should the electric power be lost if, for instance, "the big earthquake finally happens."

"It's just a matter of time," predicts Richard, noting that they are located in close proximity to both the San Jacinto and San Andreas Faults and "the big one" is about twenty years overdue.

"Ingrid runs her laundry room off of solar power and we have a battery backup system that would keep us going electrically," says Richard. "We've got three hundred gallons of propane and our own well and sewer system – we're totally self-contained except for the day-to-day electricity."

Small "earthquake storms" are common and they've felt the shake, rattle and roll of earthquakes that have torn down medium structures in the valleys below, but Richard is confident that their perch on the edge of a hill on firm rock will shield them from the more serious damage.

Always a survivalist, Richard has for years wanted to build a bomb shelter, and still has his sights set on doing just that. "There is a place in South Carolina that builds tornado shelters out of steel and has them shipped in on a truck," he says, adding that his new copper dome was shipped in from Australia.

Yes, in place of the small telescopes that the Reeves family used to pass around on starry nights as they sat outside the old bread truck and travel trailer, Richard has now built a beautiful copper dome observatory for his astronomical studies. It is seventeen feet in diameter and sits on the two and one-half acre homestead near their "stick house." Ingrid

notes that there are about eight telescopes in it. In addition to the large copper dome, Richard also has a smaller fiberglass dome up on a little knoll overlooking the homestead.

It's a far cry from that first eight-inch telescope that Ingrid bought for Richard back in 1974 shortly after they met. Never having owned a "giant one," Richard is pricing the 20-inch telescopes which run $40,000 or more. "I remember when it used to take Richard two or three hours in the afternoon or early evening to set up a telescope to track a certain star," says Ingrid. "Then, he'd spend another hour or two taking it back inside. Now he doesn't have to do that anymore. There are smart telescopes that align themselves with the push of a button, but what used to be the farming valley below us is getting too settled and we're getting secondary light from the city. The dome blocks off some of that, but not all." As with all of his projects, Richard continues to refine and perfect his dome for more intense and accurate star-gazing.

In the "old days," Richard had a broken-down Datsun that was continually being pulled over by the police for, as Wayne calls them, "fix-it tickets."

"It became a family joke," Wayne remembers. "That old Datsun was falling apart, but it was our only mode of transportation for a while."

Today, the Reeves have at least ten vehicles in the complex on their mountain, including dozers, tractors, trucks, jeeps, buses, and, best of all, the automotive "toys" that Richard and Ingrid always wanted: a 1993 Ruby Red Corvette (40th Edition) and a Radiant Radar Red 1994 Viper Roadster!

"I've always wanted a Corvette, so our first big splurge was in 1993 when we found our beautiful fortieth edition convertible," says Ingrid, adding that in 1994, she happened to be flipping through a magazine and spied the Viper.

"Oh my gosh, Richard!" she exclaimed. "I've just seen the most beautiful car I've ever seen in all my life!"

Acquiring the popular new Viper was not easy. It was an "in-demand" item and it seemed that everyone wanted at

Ingrid and Richard celebrate the acquisition of their 1994 "Radiant Radar Red" Viper Roadster

least $25,000 over the sticker price. As always, they persisted until they found a seller that was somewhat reasonable.

"His name was Norm Reeves and because he had the same last name as ours, he said he felt like he was selling his Viper to family. It's a true roadster – a two-seater that is all engine. It is not comfortable at all, but I just love the looks of the thing. We drove clear cross-country to Virginia in it for Thanksgiving a couple of years ago, and had all our clothing and accessories in zip lock bags squished around the tire in the trunk."

The Reeves keep their vehicles in a large metal building on the property. "I love owning a van, too," says Ingrid, remembering their first silver Oldsmobile van that they bought in the late 1980's about the time that they had to travel across the country when Wayne was injured at Ft. Stewart.

"We had all our bedding way in the back of the van and the backseat made into a bed. It was wonderful! We'd go 'cold-packing' with our ice chest in the back, traveling to power plants so that Richard could go to meetings. I was part of the sales team, but most of the time, Richard would go and talk technical stuff with the other engineers. He'd drop me off at the nearest park and I'd read or go dumpster diving in whatever city we were visiting. You never know what you're going to find in a dumpster – someone else's junk might be my treasure."

For example, Ingrid saved an old wicker chair from going into the dumpster one day at the dock, and, despite Richard's protests about her dumpster-diving, it has turned into his favorite patio chair.

Casting in the Pacific Ocean for the treasure of the sea

is another cherished pastime for Ingrid and for the entire Reeves family.

Their first fishing boat was a twenty-eight foot 1990 Trophy Bayliner, which was the largest towable boat you could buy without a permit. They would tow it down to Oceanside once or twice a month at least and Ingrid had a favorite fishing spot that Richard put on the coordinates.

"It was a fantastic halibut spot out in front of the San Onofre Nuclear Generating Station right down from Camp Pendleton," says Ingrid. "Jason loved fishing, too. We'd catch huge, thirty-or-forty pound halibut and they'd really put up a fight. As soon as they hit the sunlight, they'd bolt. It was a struggle to bring them in. Sometimes they'd get away. Richard devised this treble hook system so I wouldn't lose them, and I didn't. Jason teased me about my 'spiderweb' of hooks, but they worked!"

Back at the Triple R Ranch, Jason set up an area for fish-cleaning. When they brought the huge fish home on ice, he would filet them and they would have enough to feed the entire Fagawee Tribe and more.

Ingrid's secret fishing spot became off-limits after 9/11 because the waters off of Camp Pendleton were suddenly the site of daily military maneuvers.

"That's when we started docking in Los Angeles Harbor, and now we have to go out of LA Harbor to get out into the ocean," said Ingrid. "We gave the Bayliner to Jason and Chris and bought a smaller Trophy fishing boat, too. Chris owns the Bayliner and Jason owns the Trophy to this day."

The next boat they bought was a 1957 Matthews. It was an old woody – a forty-two foot sedan cruiser that reminded

Ingrid of an old Ford Thunderbird because it had the Chesapeake green top and it was white. The name of the boat when they bought it was the *Erin E* (for Elizabeth), but they renamed it the *Ingrid Yvette*.

There was an adventure early on involving the Matthews that taught Ingrid and Richard a valuable lesson.

Ling Cod that Richard caught off the Channel Islands

"We took out the boat one day – just Richard and I – to go fishing just for a little while, but it was so beautiful that we decided to go on to Catalina and stay the night. The Matthews had no generator – just batteries – and no radar system – just a ship-to-shore radio, an alarm clock and a compass."

They pulled into the harbor at Catalina and all of a sudden, the harbor master came aboard the boat. "Are you Ingrid and Richard Reeves?" he asked. "You've been reported missing. Haven't you been monitoring Channel 16? They've

been calling on the radio for you and put out a distress signal to find you."

Richard and Ingrid went ashore to tell everyone they were alright. Since then, they have always monitored Channel 16 carefully. Cary Madden, the movie producer, sold them the boat, and he was the one who reported them missing – probably worried that it wasn't as seaworthy as it should have been.

As a matter of fact, Ingrid remembers that entire outing as "the trip from hell." As they made their way back to the harbor, the fog rolled in and they could not see their hands in front of their faces. "We had no radar and we were creeping along blind when all of a sudden we heard a huge horn coming from the sky – so close that it was on top of us. It had to be from one of those big container ships. It rocked us when it passed by." Even on the trip from hell, Ingrid's angels surrounded them in a circle of protective love, and they came to no harm.

Their current forty-two-foot 1972 Grand Banks Fishing Trawler, the *Alegria* (Spanish for "Jubilant and Joyful"), sits idly at the dock most of the time, awaiting its owners, who remain too busy to spend as much time on it as they would like.

"We haven't gone out on the boat since last summer," lamented Ingrid on a day in July of 2010.

"We just go down and visit it for a couple of hours once in a while, just to make sure it is still afloat. Richard, being a Navy man, knows how to sail a boat. He's a good captain and he'll be the one to take it in and out of the slip. I won't steer it unless we're out in the ocean."

The last time they took out the *Alegria*, they went to Isthmus Two Harbors in Catalina with Richard's best friend,

The Alegria

Ralph Eger, and his wife, Carol, and spent the night on the boat.

"It's quiet and not as touristy as Avalon," said Ingrid. "We fished and I blew bubbles and saw dolphins, but it was so hot that it became unbearable and we went back to L.A. Harbor the next day."

As to the dolphins, Ingrid insists that she sees them every time they go out on the boat. "I think they sense that I am there," she says. "I've always been an animal healer and they know who I am. Richard will be up on the helm captaining the boat and I'll tell him I'm going to call in my babies. I say, 'Okay, Mama's here. Time to come see me – time to play!' Pretty soon, he'll shout 'Your babies are coming!' They ride the wake of the boat and they are so beautiful."

When they have company on board, or even when it is

just the two of them, Ingrid is in charge of the galley. “I still use the treble hook and I always cook the fish we catch,” she says. “I filet them if we have a bunch and put them in the freezer. During lobster season, we’ll have a lobster boil. I fix burritos, steak, baked potatoes and green beans, grilled cheese sandwiches, peanut butter and jelly sandwiches, nuts and popcorn. I fix eggs, turkey sausage and hash browns for breakfast. We mostly drink water and iced tea, although Richard still likes his coffee and, occasionally, a Miller Lite Beer.”

Because it is a 1972 model, the *Alegria* is set up for men, with single bunks in the two staterooms and a couch in the salon. On the bottom deck is Ingrid’s favorite place on the boat – the engine room. “The engine room is Richard’s realm. It is an awesome, spotless place and I love to look in, but don’t spend much time in there.”

As often happens to the things that Ingrid loves, the beautiful old Matthews woody has remained in the family. Today, it sits on their property on the mountain and is slated to become a unique reading room.

“Yard art!” declares Ingrid. “We’re going to build a little dock around it and make it look like it is floating in the ocean. It feels good to go aboard her. After all, she was my first Dream Boat. Richard will put up a little sign in front that says, *‘Damn the boulders! Full speed ahead!’*”

The Matthews fishing boat is just one example of the “yard art” gathered around the old Reeves homestead and surrounding property. Jason, who lives on the property with his family, has a collection of Ford Mustangs. He builds them from the frame up and keeps them parked there for parts.

“He has spent a great deal of good quality time with his

children working on cars," said Ingrid, adding that Chris collected and restored Volkswagen buses ("hippie buses") before he moved to Colorado, and the "neighbor from hell" called the county and complained.

"So, now, we're not allowed to have any cars on the property that don't run. They have to be licensed and running, which I feel is ridiculous," declared Ingrid. "What better pastime is there for a father and his children, than to work on restoring old cars?"

Old cars and boats are kept and cherished at the Reeves homestead, as are a large number of antiques that Richard and Ingrid have collected over the years. When they first moved to their mountain, they would go to swap meets and buy things they needed because that was the least expensive way to get good quality. They often ran into antiques at the swap meets and both of them developed a love and respect for the beautifully hand-crafted, one-of-a-kind century-old furnishings and accessories.

"Everything we bought had to have a use," Ingrid says, "and no matter how valuable an antique, we used it." Ingrid and Cher used to go shopping for antiques, even before she met Richard. Cher would call and tell Ingrid there was a garage sale going on, and off they'd go. For example, there is the little chest of drawers with heart-shaped glove boxes made of oak. "People used to wear these long gloves and store them in the heart-shaped glove boxes," explains Ingrid. "I paid $200 for it in 1970 and still use it to this day."

Cher was an even more avid antique collector than Ingrid and, at one time, she had an entire house loaded with antique toys, including carousel horses, but that house was

consumed in flames during one of the fires that so often rage through the Southern California hills.

In Ingrid and Richard's "stick house," there is an 1800's room that has some special antiques in it, including Ingrid's ocean-blue wood-burning cook stove with the heart handles.

In the 1800's room, there is also a little 1736 loveseat with claw-foot legs and horse hair in it that Ingrid bought for $600.

"Richard never complained when I wanted to buy an antique," recalls Ingrid. "I'd always tell him 'I really want this,' and we'd talk about it together before we bought anything to see if we could afford it." Today, they can afford to buy whatever antique suits their fancy, but being practical folks, they rarely go antiquing anymore. They've pretty much got what they need, and that's one another.

"We're still almost like one," muses Ingrid. "We still talk about everything together. Neither of us had anything when we met. He had the old "Love Bug" and I had nothing. We just worked and worked and grew together."

Working, clearing land, raising kids, building a business – nearly always together – once in a while, even 24/7 workaholics need to take a break, and Ingrid does that every few years when her alma mater, Bloomington High School, has a class reunion. Richard is not interested in partying the night away with Ingrid's old classmates, but she has rarely, if ever, missed a reunion. "I have a blast!" she declares.

At the summer of 2010's forty-fifth reunion of the classes of 1965 to 1975, Ingrid met her two old friends, Carol and Carol, at Fairmont Park in Riverside where they enjoyed a marvelous picnic beneath a huge oak tree and then danced the evening away at a nearby hall. "I won the hula hoop!" Ingrid exclaims with delight.

Jerry Bailey of San Bernardino, California, was in the Bloomington High School Class of 1968, a couple of years after Ingrid, but he remembers her well from high school and, of course, from the many reunions they've shared.

"Ingrid was a great cheerleader in high school and she hasn't changed one bit," said Bailey. "She's still a cheerleader!" Bailey notes that from the time the reunions start until they are finished, Ingrid dances. "If she didn't show up, it wouldn't be the same," he said. "She's the life of the party!"

Despite Ingrid's solo dancing at reunions, she and Richard have enjoyed some great recreational pursuits together as well. Back in the 1980's, when Richard was still working for E. C. deYoung in Riverside, he and Ingrid had taken their little camp trailer to McGrath State Park where work was being done on the Mandalay Generating Station. It was there they happened to find a brand new hobby.

"It was one of the worker's birthdays and we all went out for his birthday to a little bar named Murphy's," recalls Ingrid. "The guys were playing pool and there was a dart board over there, so I started throwing darts. Then a fight broke out and pool balls were being thrown all of a sudden! I ended up grabbing guys on our crew by the t-shirts and pulling them out of the bar. That was the first time I ever played darts, but it was too short a time."

After that memorable introduction to darts, Ingrid couldn't wait to get to a calm dart game and try her luck again. She was thrilled to find out that there were dart leagues in the area and she and Richard joined a dart team at Hamby's in Hemet, California.

Another darts tournament trophy, 1987

"Richard was an absolute natural at darts. We played as a husband and wife team all through the 1980's at Hamby's in the closest little town to us. At the time, we played on a league called the Inland Valley Darts Association, traveling to tournaments all over California and into Nevada on weekends. We won all kinds of plaques and trophies. I was good, but not anywhere near as good as Richard. There was one year when Richard was teamed up in a televised dart game in Vegas with Paul Lim at the North American Pro-Am. Paul Lim was the top steel-tip dart thrower in the nation. It was exciting – you never knew what would happen next – and we enjoyed the competition, but we finally had to stop because the heavy smoke in the bars really got to us. I can't take the smoke."

Once during those years, the Reeves really splurged and accepted an invitation from Doug Hamby (the owner of Hamby's) to join him on his time-share houseboat, *The Dawn Threader*, and sail Lake Powell near the Zion National Park in Utah.

Doug told them it was going to be all couples, but it turned out that Ingrid and her cousin, Brenda, were the only two women and there were nine men.

"We were afraid we'd be galley slaves, but it turned out great," declares Ingrid. "All the men chipped in cooking and we spent Father's Day aboard and they all called their dads ship-to-shore. It was an awesome trip." One day, she remembers, the younger men bought fruit for daiquiris, put on tuxedo ties and swimming suits and acted like the Chippendale dancers while serving the two women fruit drinks with little umbrellas in them.

"We spent a glorious seven days aboard that big old houseboat," recalls Ingrid, "and we went up all the arms of the lake, with Richard as the navigator on Doug's little sea boat, *The Emotional Rescue*. Richard and I fished from the house-boat and the guys mostly went water skiing. It was a beautiful vacation, especially when Richard dove in and brought me back a treasure. We were standing on this bluff looking out into the water and he saw something sparkling on a ledge about ten feet down. He dove in and it was an Indian silver and turquoise ring with a leaf on it. If he had knocked it just a little, it would have fallen hundreds of feet. I still wear it on my pinky."

As for other trips and travels during those business-building years of the 1980's, there was the Reeves' trip to Austria that resulted from Ingrid's once-in-a-lifetime win on the television show, *The Price is Right*. Richard's cousin, Cliff, and his wife, Jackie, had tickets to the show, starring Bob Barker. At the time that Ingrid accompanied them, Richard stayed behind at the ranch with a broken ankle.

"I was the fourth one they interviewed in line," recalls Ingrid. "They tell you to start talking and I said, 'Well, my husband is home with a broken ankle.' I got picked as a contestant and went all the way to the showcase!"

The first thing Ingrid had to do was guess the right price of a diamond-studded necklace. She guessed the right price and was invited on stage, winning a trip to Austria that included five days at the Hilton Hotel.

"Richard and I went to Austria," she recalls. "We didn't have much money at the time, and I remember we went to the bunkers where Hitler had been, and to a park with a huge Ferris wheel that had a big globe of the earth in the middle, and we went to a winery that was run by nuns. They made and sold their own wine and I wanted to buy some red wine, but they wanted me to buy white wine. We bought one little bottle. Richard and I drank some of it and I lost a whole day. The wine was so strong, it wiped me out."

The memories make her smile. Sparkling vignettes of days gone by … they dance through her mind, just as bubbles blown from the boat dance across the surface of the water.

Love, sunshine and bubbles … when the bubbles glint in the sunshine, they look like rainbows. If you soap up your hands and catch the bubbles, you can pile them one on top of the other and they become one, just like memories. Today, Ingrid can share the magic of bubbles with her youngest grandson, Preston True, but even with the love of family, the sunshine of prosperity and the beautiful bubbles of memories, Ingrid spends the majority of her time as she has spent it all of her life – working.

Until 2010, Ingrid did all the paperwork, all the taxes, all the payroll for the company – and she did it all by hand, with no use of computers. Finally, in 2010, their tax man did the payroll, but Ingrid continued to drive parts to various jobs, and run from task to task. Richard continued to do the work of five people in engineering, and Jason began to follow in his footsteps. Both were still working full-time, but Ingrid and Richard had reached a great point in their lives where they were financially secure, and retirement was actually in sight!

"We have a tiny post office in Homeland that used to be run by Hugo, who had been there about the same time we've been on our property – thirty-three years," says Ingrid. "Hugo's not there anymore, but he used to always tell everybody how proud he was of our accomplishments. He knew how we started out. He'd say, 'These are my prize people. They started with nothing and worked so hard and look at them now!'"

Now is very nice. Next year will be even better. If Ingrid has her way, every year will mark an increase of love, sunshine and bubbles and a decrease of work, work, work. With her soul-mate by her side, her successful business, her stick house, dream cars, boulders, boats, antiques and her family, friends and high school classmates – Ingrid finally has time and means to do some of the spiritual exploration she has always dreamed of doing.

On her sixtieth birthday – January 24, 2007, Wayne and his wife, Shirley (who adores her mother-in-law), teamed up and put their feelings into words into a lovely birthday poem for Ingrid. Wayne calls Ingrid "Mums" because of his Trinidad heritage on her side of the family. Ingrid still treasures the pretty card that held the following "Birthday Poem for Mums."

One's sense of self-worth
Evolves from the moment of birth.
It is perception learned,
Although not easily discerned.
It is influenced by experiences of life,
And exposure to trials and strife.
But the greatest of factors,
Is the guidance of good mothers.
This seems especially true,
When, Mums, I remember you.
Your love and wisdom
Gave me strength to overcome.
I know, now, that you felt
My childhood fears and doubt.
Mutual respect and etiquette I value,
Because of good manners learned from you.
I recall you working hour after hour,
And doing everything in your power,
To fill our closets and cupboard
With the most you could afford.
You did your best to provide,
To love your children, and to guide.
So, in honor of your special day,
Please allow me to say,
Thanks, Mums,
For all you've done.
With Love from,
Wayne, your son.

Ingrid's sixth decade of life has been one of spiritual exploration and discovery and, while Richard laughingly stays at arm's length from the psychic cruises and seminars that so fascinate his wife, he supports Ingrid in her quest for answers just as she supports him in his star-gazing. Already a world traveler by 2007, Ingrid chose that year to begin sailing on psychic cruises that would take her to a new world of the spirit. She has continued exploring that new world and its infinite possibilities.

Ingrid is cruising toward the next big adventure of her life … a sacred mountain sanctuary and healing center called the Circle of Love, but first, she invites you, in Chapter 9, to join her on a few of those fabulous, life-enhancing cruises.

Chapter 9

"Woo-Woo" Cruises

Richard jokes about Ingrid's spiritual awakening, calling it her "woo-woo stuff." He once told a neighbor that since Ingrid got into the world of psychic cruises, intuitive exploration and mystical discovery, "you can't find a live chicken anywhere in the neighborhood."

Ingrid just grins. "Richard thinks he's sooooo funny," she says, her sapphire eyes brimming with love, her joyful sense of humor as deep as her pretty dimples.

Ingrid's journey to spiritual enlightenment has been a long one. From that first frightening glimpse of the huge crucifix on her mother's bedroom wall through a lifetime spent seeking God's truth, Ingrid has evolved into a deep thinker, a powerful healer. A spirit-filled woman of such purity, strength and joy, she is instinctively recognized by others who have achieved that same level of enlightenment.

For instance, on a life-altering cruise to Alaska in 2009, Ingrid was acknowledged as a shaman by the ancient master carver of the totem poles in Ketchikan.

"He speaks to no one," the tour bus driver whispered in awe as Ingrid innocently related the nice conversation she had just had with the old man in the silent, heavily mystical, other-worldly "carving place" – a room with a dirt floor covered by cedar and spruce shavings, reeking of an earthy mix of forest and human odors … sweat, blood, feathers and fur … where few voices are ever heard.

When Ingrid's pure, sweet voice broke the silence in the carving place, all heads turned. The ancient one smiled at her and paused in his carving to answer her questions. All eyes widened in astonishment.

"I told him that I was in search of a shaman totem pole," she recalls. "He looked at me long and hard and then he said that shaman totem poles were rare and not available for sale. I asked him if there were any books about the shaman totem poles and he gave me the name of one that I was never able to find. We connected – the two of us. I knew he was a shaman and he knew I was one."

For as far back as she can remember, Ingrid has felt an innate ability to channel God's healing power through her touch.

"Animals have always sensed it in me and I can't tell you how many thorns I've removed from festering paws; how many lame, four-legged creatures have found me and run off healed … it's not always God's will that something or someone will heal, but when it is, I can feel the healing happen."

Her healing has evolved over the years into a simple and extremely powerful ritual, as follows:

> *"What I do is I place my hand on the spot of the ailment and I ask Mother God, Father God, Jesus and all the angels to help me, if it is their will, and use me as a vessel to pour out healing on the person I'm touching. We both close our eyes and I tell the person to visualize a big red ball and to stuff all of that cancer or pain or whatever is ailing them into that ball. I ask them to concentrate on stuffing everything that hurts into it until it is full, full, full. Then we both visualize placing that ball into a clear acrylic cube and shooting that cube up into the universe into a black hole – an infinite event horizon – never to return – gone – obliterated forever."*

Often, this healing ritual works. Sometimes, Ingrid notes, if the Gods and angels deem that this person needs to go through this and can't be healed, there is at least a sense of peace and well-being that can be achieved through the red ball meditation. One thing that Ingrid always emphasizes to anyone she seeks to heal is that it is simply a supplement to medical treatment.

"Nothing replaces a medical doctor," she says, "and I always make that very clear. The red ball is just one more circle in the ongoing circle of love in my life."

Why the red ball? "All my life, when I was just doodling, I always drew a clear cubicle with a red ball in it," says Ingrid. "To me, the red ball is all the trouble, and the cube is the power of God to trap it and make sure the trouble stays gone."

Although she has had this strong penchant for visualization and healing since early childhood, Ingrid has rarely had time in her busy life to dwell on it … until now.

"Little by little, Richard and I began delegating the work to Jason and his crew and aiming toward retirement," notes Ingrid. "And, I started early, doing some fun things just for me. "

While Richard prefers to stay back on "the farm" and pursue his astronomy, keeping his finger on the pulse of the company and feeding the animals that seem determined to take up residence there, Ingrid adores getting totally away from the heavy responsibility that has been hers for so long. Nothing takes her farther away, both physically and emotionally, than a cruise. And, as long as the cruise takes her away from Richard for no more than seven days, Ingrid is ready to go at the drop of her pink hardhat!

"I'd love it if Richard would go with me, but he doesn't enjoy cruising. Even the few times he has gone in the past, he stayed in our stateroom the whole time, so he didn't really enjoy himself, but I loved it that he was there – just so I could go sit and watch the stars with him and check on him," says Ingrid.

"Richard is a very private man who enjoys the peace and quiet of our mountain – we enjoy it together, but I also want to travel. I hate to leave him alone. I hate not to go. So

I've compromised by promising myself and him that I won't leave him for more than seven days at a time."

Ingrid's lifetime interest in psychic phenomenon and spirituality was refreshed the first time she saw Sylvia Browne on the Montel Williams Show in late 2007.

"I rarely have time to watch television, but I was stopped in my tracks by Sylvia Browne one day. At first, I thought, ooh, she sounds interesting … then when I took a closer look at the screen, I wasn't too sure about her. She had the longest fingernails I'd ever seen and when I saw them curling around, all I could think of was 'how in the world does she stay clean?'"

Just weeks after that first television encounter with Browne, Ingrid was walking through WalMart when "one of Sylvia Browne's books jumped out at me!" Later, when Enid was visiting, they went to the Pala Casino and there was Sylvia Browne!

Montel, Ingrid and Sylvia Browne

"Enid loves to gamble and there is no gambling in Hawaii, so when she comes here, I take her to the casinos and get her a room. While she gambles, I go to the shows," said Ingrid. "Sylvia Browne was the show, and both Enid and I enjoyed her. That's when we heard about the psychic cruises."

It was in July of 2008 that Ingrid first took Enid on a Sylvia Browne cruise to Mexico for her July 10th birthday. Enid won a half-hour reading with Sylvia, and everybody on the cruise was allowed to ask her one question.

At the time, Ingrid still believed that Walter Marcus was her father. "I told Sylvia Browne that I had never met my grandparents because they were both killed in a concentration camp, and that I knew my grandfather's name was Max, but I never knew my grandmother's name," remembers Ingrid. "The strange thing was that Sylvia really hesitated when I mentioned my dad, Walter. Then she said, 'Oh, oh, oh yeah. His mother was a sweet little lady named Esther.'"

Sylvia Browne also taught the cruisers how to meditate. Ingrid loved the mystical part of the cruise and attended every session, absorbing all of the teachings, and the rest of the time, she spent actively enjoying the cruise activities. She did karaoke, contests, miniature golf, and danced nightly until the dance floor was empty.

"I'd find my dancing spot and dance by myself every single dance," she says. "I don't dance with men. Richard is my man. But, oh, the music goes right through me and dancing to it gives me such joy that I dance like there's no tomorrow. I twirl like nobody is watching."

Richard had asked her not to get off the ship in Mexico because of the rampant crime and violence in that country, and

Ingrid respected that request, staying on the ship at Cancun and Mazatlan.

Although she didn't get a reading with Sylvia on that first cruise, Ingrid did schedule one with the beautiful, Celtic-looking psychic Colette Baron-Reid.

Ingrid and Colette Baron-Reid

"Colette told me that she had a horrific childhood – even worse than mine," Ingrid recalls. "She was gang-raped as a teenager and so was her mother when she was nineteen back in Germany during the war. Colette always knew she was an intuitive. She has written several books, too. I was actually glad that Sylvia was booked, because Colette's reading was meant to be for me."

Colette had a very soft suede bag full of ancient Greek rune stones. She told Ingrid to reach in the bag and pull out five of them. When she put the stones on the table, Colette was shocked. "She jumped up and the words started pouring out of her. She said, 'You are shaman status! You could be doing what I'm doing and making money at it. You've got to study reiki … you're a natural healer … you're amazing!'"

Ingrid had always sensed that she had healing powers within her, but it was when Colette told her that Walter was not her biological father that she realized this was a life-changing reading.

Colette told her, in great detail, that she was the result of a one-night stand at the serviceman's club in Trinidad; that her biological father was a Nordic Irishman, not Walter Marcus. "My older sister, Dee, confirmed that later," recalls Ingrid. "She said, 'Oh, we always knew Walter wasn't your real dad,' but it came as a shock to me, even though I'd had my suspicions about it all my life."

When Ingrid told Colette that she had been scared to death of her mother, Colette nodded with understanding and informed Ingrid that she had a right to be terrified of her mother; that her mother had been raped repeatedly as a child and had such anger inside her that she would have slit a man's throat in an instant.

"That's when I forgave my mother," recalls Ingrid. "Mom passed away in 1992 and I was still afraid of her, but I loved her, too."

The reading with Colette opened up a whole new world for Ingrid – a world that she wanted to pursue with the same vigor that she had poured into working all of her life. In fact, Colette warned Ingrid that she needed to stop being a workaholic or risk being deathly ill. Although that is easier said than done, Ingrid has since then "worked hard at not working as hard."

Cruising was one way to get away from all that hard work, and since that first mystical cruise in July of 2008, Ingrid has embarked on several enjoyable cruises. She took a four-night Pacific Coast Cruise with Dr. Laura Schlesinger in September of 2008 on Holland America Lines – Vancouver to San Diego – and another Mystical Traveler Cruise to the Mexican Riviera with Sylvia Browne and Colette Baron-Reid in April of 2009 aboard the Emerald Princess.

Something incredible happened on the Emerald Princess that would ultimately have a life-changing effect on Ingrid.

Just as Sylvia Browne's appearance on television had stopped her in her tracks and eventually led her on a path of psychic cruises toward self-discovery and spiritual growth, a painting in the ship's gallery by internationally famous U.K. artist Josephine Wall absolutely knocked Ingrid to the floor.

Having missed the art auction, Ingrid was simply strolling through the gallery to catch a glimpse of the pretty paintings when she got zapped.

"I walked past *Crystal of Enchantment* and stopped and turned around and walked back," recalls Ingrid. "It was the most beautiful painting I'd ever seen in my life."

So stunned was she by the beauty of the painting that she literally sank to the floor and sat there, contemplating the painting for half an hour or more.

The lady in the painting was blonde and bore a remarkable resemblance to Ingrid, but there was much more than that to the attraction she felt. "I saw the faces in it – the same faces I'd been seeing everywhere all my life!" exclaims Ingrid. "Somehow, the artist of this painting had put my imagination on canvas … all the beautiful, sparkling colors, all the joyful feelings, the butterflies, shells, sunbeams, and the tiny faces of angels … there were even hummingbirds like the ones that Richard and I nurture on our mountain, and a gramophone playing the music I've heard in my mind for years … everything I had seen in my head and heard with my heart was there in front of my eyes!"

Crystal of Enchantment
by Josephine Wall

Ingrid asked the gallery curator for the name of the artist and he told her the name of a man he thought had painted the painting.

"No way!" responded Ingrid. "There is no way a man painted this painting!"

Instinctively identifying with the absolute beauty and innocence of the lady holding the *Crystal of Enchantment* in her hand, Ingrid knew the artist was a woman and she knew she had to have that painting.

Smugly, the curator informed her that the art auction

was over and the painting was not for sale. No amount of persuasion would sway him, and finally, Ingrid left the gallery carrying nothing but the image of *Crystal of Enchantment* in her mind and her heart.

A woman of great determination and one who has also learned patience over a lifetime of working for and waiting for what she wants, Ingrid knew that she would eventually own that painting. She did not know, at the time, the incredible significance that Josephine Wall and her spirit of imagination art would have in her future.

About a week after arriving home from the cruise on the Emerald Princess, Ingrid went to a doctor's appointment in Loma Linda and, before driving home, stopped to pick up a few things at her favorite health food store, Clark's Nutrition. Sparkling on a card rack at Clark's, was Josephine Wall's *Crystal of Enchantment*!

"Oh, my gosh!" she exclaimed. "My painting!"

In fact, that painting was one of several images by Josephine Wall that appeared on greeting cards at Clark's. There was a whole package of the artist's cards for $20, and Ingrid bought the package, absorbing the beautiful images one after another, completely amazed at the work of Josephine Wall. The lyrical, romantic images leapt out at her and captured her imagination, but none so strongly as *Crystal of Enchantment*. She turned the card box over and found a phone number for Leanin' Tree. The man who answered the phone at Leanin' Tree Cards instructed Ingrid to go on-line in order to get in touch with the representative of Josephine Wall's art. He gave her the website and email address.

"I told him I don't use computers, and I guess he felt

sorry for me," says Ingrid, grinning. "He gave me Pat Sager's phone number. Pat was astonished when I called her direct, but it didn't take long for her to know it was meant to be that we have that conversation."

Dr. Pat Sager, Josephine Wall's International Marketing Director and U.S. Event Coordinator, identified instantly with Ingrid. The Regional Director of Webster University for twenty-nine years, Pat had been on a cruise in 2005 when she encountered Josephine Wall's art.

"I have never been an art collector, unless it had to do with collecting fancy costumes for fairy and renaissance fairs and Star Trek memorabilia as a devoted Trekkie," Pat admits, "but Jo Wall's painting, *Iris, Keeper of the Rainbow*, spoke to me on a cruise just like *Crystal of Enchantment* spoke to Ingrid. I was so stunned by Jo's art that I could not leave the ship without owning at least two of her paintings."

In addition to *Iris, Keeper of the Rainbow*, Pat also purchased *Minerva's Melody*, and immediately set about making plans to meet the artist personally. Pat had been on a quest for the new direction she would take following her retirement from Webster University, and now, after experiencing the spirit of imagination art created by Josephine Wall, she knew what she was going to do.

"When I first saw Jo's fabulous paintings, I thought I must be dreaming," recalls Pat. "It was art unlike anything I had ever seen except in my own fantasy dreams, and then I realized that it was the art of my fantasy dreams and I had found it. Jo's incredible art was exactly what I had been looking for all my life."

In 2007, after meeting Jo Wall at a fairy festival and

confirming that this was, indeed, her destiny, Pat Sager retired and took on her new role of promoting Jo's art and all the products from her images as Jo's authorized exclusive international internet sales distributor. Soon, Pat had opened an e-commerce website (www.josephine-wall-imagination-art.com) with a link to Josephine Wall's own website (www.josephinewall.com).

But, of course, all of these websites and email addresses meant absolutely nothing to Ingrid, and as she explained at length to Pat about how she had found the painting on the psychic cruise; how she just knew it wasn't painted by a man; how she'd found it again on a card at Clark's Nutrition store; and how she was determined to own the painting, whatever it took, but she didn't do email, etc., etc., etc., the conversation somehow evolved into a discussion between friends.

"Pat was completely in tune with me spiritually, and she wanted to know all about the psychic cruises and all about me. We felt a connection right away. It was like she was my kindred spirit – a long-lost baby sister. We melded perfectly on the spirituality stuff. We talked like we'd known each other all our lives."

As to Ingrid acquiring *Crystal of Enchantment*, that remained a problem. Immediately after receiving Ingrid's call, Pat got in touch with Josephine Wall in the U.K. and asked about getting a print shipped to Ingrid in California. No deal, Jo told Pat. She had an arrangement with the cruise lines and could not sell those paintings elsewhere, so Ingrid would just have to go on another cruise to get that particular painting. Jo was adamant. A contract was a contract, and other than those on the high seas, there were no other prints available of *Crystal of Enchantment.*

"You can't imagine how hard it was for me to call Ingrid back and tell her that the print was not available and that Jo suggested she go on another cruise to get one," says Pat. "What amazed me was that Ingrid just said okay, with a smile in her voice. What a sweet lady she is!"

And sure enough, in July of 2009, Ingrid and Enid once again took a cruise to celebrate Enid's birthday – this time on Holland America's MS Amsterdam sailing from Seattle, Washington to Alaska. Sponsored by Hay House Publishers, it was called the "I Can Do It" At Sea Cruise, and featured a wide array of authors, inspirational speakers, psychics and intuitives, including Dr. Wayne W. Dyer, Sylvia Browne, Caroline Myss, Cheryl Richardson, Dr. Brian Weiss, Colette Baron-Reid, Gregg Braden, John Holland, Sonia Choquette, Iyanla Vanzant, Lisa Fugard, Reid Tracy, and Margarete Nielsen.

Sailing to Juneau, Sitka and Ketchikan, with marvelous sessions and events happening both on board ship and at port, Ingrid had the time of her life in Alaska.

"I loved Alaska!" she exclaims. "Magical things happened nearly every time I stepped off the boat. It was a beautiful time of awakening for me. In fact, when I look at the pictures we took that week, there are orbs floating all around me in nearly every picture. The spirits danced with me the whole time."

In Ketchikan, they went to see the totem poles and Ingrid joined the Eskimo dancers, becoming one with the music and the ritual. Of all the dancers in the circle, they chose Ingrid to be the one on whom they draped the sacred robe.

"It was lovely silk, heavy and embroidered with all of my beautiful purples, yellows, blues and greens," recalls Ingrid. "When they put it on me, I could feel the magic go through me, and it stayed with me even when the robe was removed. I felt like it was still on me."

At one point while she was visiting the totem pole area, a huge Alaskan sled dog came running up to Ingrid, wrapped his paws around her neck and hugged her, licking all over her face like he recognized her. "He was a great big beautiful Husky with blue eyes – more wolf than dog – and all of the locals were asking, 'Where did he come from? What's he doing here? Why is he running around loose?' As soon as he greeted me, he walked away."

Another mysterious thing happened when Ingrid was in Ketchikan. Colette had told her to find a quiet spot where she could see the icebergs breaking up and to look for a message from the ice. Ingrid found a quiet corner away from the crowd and stood silently watching the ice floating down into the water.

"All of a sudden, a big hunk of ice broke off and crashed into the water!" she recalls. "I saw an ancient Eskimo face in the ice and heard chanting that sounded like 'Wah-ahoo! Wah-ahoo! Wah-ahoo!' I turned around because I thought some kids must be behind me goofing off and making that chanting noise, but there was no one there. It was a voice that I heard coming from the ice – coming from that ancient Eskimo face in the ice. I knew it was my shaman and I started looking for him in the totem poles and everywhere."

Later, after being told by the totem pole carving master that there were no shaman totem poles for sale, Ingrid found the exact face she had seen in the ice, but it was not on a totem pole – instead, it was on a necklace carved out of caribou. "Oh my God, I found him!" she exclaimed, claiming the necklace (with earrings to match) as her own personal Alaskan totem.

In researching the history of totem poles and her own spiritual totems, Ingrid has gained deeper understanding of their mystical pull on her heart.

A totem is a symbol of a tribe, clan, family or individual. In the ancient tribal traditions of Alaska and North America, the legend is that each individual is connected with at least nine different animals that will act as guides throughout life. Different animal guides enter our lives at different times depending on our direction and the tasks ahead of us. For

Ingrid, who has had a special bond with animals all her life, the totem is a sacred symbol indeed.

The original carvers of totem poles lived in what is now known as Alaska's Inside Passage, being members of the Tlingit, Haida and other clans of Southwest Alaska.

Primarily, the symbols carved into the totem poles represent their specific clan. Tradition has it that at the highest level, every individual is either of the eagle or the raven clan, with sub-clans such as beaver, fox, bear, frog, buffalo, deer, crocodile, dog, etc. Nearly always, the human figure at the top of a totem pole symbolizes the village watchman, who warns the villagers of approaching danger or a thief in their midst.

In some very rare old totem poles, figures can be found that are carved upside down in the wood. This symbolized that the figure owed a debt to the village. Once the debt was paid, the pole would be chopped down and taken into the forest to rot, and a new one would be erected. Red ears and mouth signify a stingy person, and, surprisingly, the "low man on the totem pole" is often the most important.

Among the various types of Alaskan (and Native North American Indian) totem poles are:

<u>Crest Totem Poles</u> – usually built into the house structure, portraying the family's history and clan emblem.

<u>Story-telling Totem Poles</u> – the most common type – made for weddings, to preserve history or to ridicule bad debtors.

<u>Mortuary Totem Poles</u> – to honor the dead. Sometimes cremation ashes are kept in a compartment within the carved totem pole, and one single figure represents the deceased person or their clan.

Usually made of spruce or cedar, the totem poles are traditionally carved by adzes (sharp blades tied to wooden handles). Two larger adzes are used to remove big pieces of wood from the bare tree trunk and an elbow adze (so-called because of its similarity in appearance to the human elbow) is used for final shaping. Today's professional native carvers, such as those Ingrid met in the special carving place in Ketchikan, may charge as much as $3,000 per foot to carve an authentic totem pole.

Black, red, brown and blue-green are the predominant colors found on totem poles and the paints are traditionally made by mixing charcoal, cinnabar (mercury ore), iron oxide and copper oxide with oil from salmon eggs.

Raising the totem pole is a sacred ceremony that involves hard work on the part of the villagers. Once a hole has been dug, tribal members carry the finished totem pole to the site and it is pulled upright with ropes amid a celebration of drumming, dancing and singing.

Often, legend has it, the sacred raven or brave eagle will be seen soaring over the site of a totem pole raising, which is a sign of mystical approval.

In the painting, *Sacred Places*, by Alaskan artist Skye Ryan-Evans, the eagle soars over an ancient totem pole high in the mountains as the wolf totem further blesses the spirit.

For Ingrid, the Alaskan cruise was, indeed, a time of spiritual sanctity and awakening that culminated in two extremely meaningful and life-changing events. First, Ingrid got a reading done by Sylvia Browne and revealed to Sylvia a deep-down feeling she has finally allowed to surface.

"I told Sylvia that I believe I walked in Jesus' time

and that I knew him as a brother," says Ingrid. "Sylvia confirmed that I did walk with him and that I was, in fact, a Gnostic teacher and knew Jesus and Mary Magdalene and their children. She was in a trance as she talked of the bloodline of Jesus and Mary and how it had come down through the centuries to one of the Catholic popes. She talked of an important message to the world that is buried under the feet of the Sphinx over in Egypt. The reading only lasted twenty minutes, and at the very end of it, I asked her the name of my biological father and she said he was a Nordic Irishman named Robert."

The reading with Sylvia confirmed some of Ingrid's long-time theories of Mother God, Father God and Jesus as Brother God. Also, without being given any prior information, Sylvia confirmed that Ingrid's father was, as Colette and her older sister, Dee, had said, a Nordic Irishman.

"This explained a lot for me about my fair skin and blonde hair as a child," says Ingrid. "I feel that my mother knew all along, and that was one of the reasons she abused me so badly. I was the result of a one-night stand. I really was different from all the others.

Cruisin'

As Ingrid dances,
three orbs surround her!

Chapter 10

Jo Wall's "Spirit of Imagination" Art

Ingrid had just one regret about her marvelous mystical Alaskan cruise … the art auction had featured none of Josephine Wall's art and she was still without her *Crystal of Enchantment.*

Ingrid's quest for the painting had by now become Pat's quest, too. Back and forth, the calls flew fast and furious from Florida to California to Florida, and back to Wisteria Cottage in Dorset, England where Jo and her husband, Bob, reside. But, it seemed, the calls were all to no avail. The painting was available only on cruises.

Not to worry, Ingrid assured Pat. She and Enid had another psychic cruise lined up in November of 2009… maybe the painting would be on this one!

After more than six months of long, heart-felt phone calls from California, Pat was becoming so enthralled with

Ingrid's stories of the psychic cruises that she had started saving money toward booking a cruise herself.

When Enid had to cancel at the last minute due to illness (which, unfortunately, was eventually diagnosed as cancer of the larynx, but is now in remission), Ingrid invited Pat to accompany her on the cruise. Her only criterion for taking this virtual stranger on a seven-day Holland America cruise to the Caribbean was that Pat not smoke. That was an easy one, as Pat is not a smoker and smoke bothers her as much as it does Ingrid.

"I was so thrilled," recalls Pat. "The cruise embarked from Ft. Lauderdale on November 7th and my birthday is November 10th. It was a dream come true!"

When Pat picked Ingrid up at the airport in Fort Lauderdale on November 7, 2009, it was their first face-to-face meeting.

"When I saw Pat for the first time, I thought she was stunning," recalls Ingrid. "This woman had such an hourglass figure, I felt like humpty-dumpty! Pat looked like a beautiful fairy to me – my mischievous angel – my little sister in another life. We picked up right where we left off in our last phone conversation."

Sharing a stateroom on a seven-day cruise can be challenging even for two people who know one another well. For Pat and Ingrid, it was a delightful learning experience.

"Pat is so very much fun. She's very intellectual and interesting," recalls Ingrid. It didn't take long for the two cruisers to adjust to their differences while celebrating their similarities. For instance, Ingrid is extremely punctual and Pat is not.

"I don't like to be late, and so I just started telling Pat that I'd go on ahead and meet her. I like to sit up front at the lectures so that I can hear and see everything. Pat usually comes in ten or fifteen minutes late. That's okay. She is who she is and I am who I am. We worked out our own schedules." Ingrid loved going dancing every night and would find her space on the dance floor and dance until three or four in the morning and then go out on the veranda and gaze at the stars. One night, Pat got up and came out to join her as she was star-gazing.

"What are you doing?" she asked Ingrid. "I'm waiting for a meteor shower," Ingrid replied. Pat waited with her and soon, they were witnessing a lovely meteor shower.

"That looked like a shooting star!" shouted Pat. "That was a meteor shower," explained Ingrid, amazed that Pat had never seen one in her life, and thrilled that she was seeing her very first one that night.

"Looking at the sky is something I must do every day and every night if the weather is clear," said Ingrid. "It was a new experience for Pat, who is not outdoorsy, but an educator and a scholar."

The meteor shower was just one example of how two very different personalities could come together in such incredible harmony. "Pat learned to enjoy looking up at the sky more often and I learned a lot of insights from her, too. I love sunrise on the ship and once in a while, she'd be up to see her sunbeams. She'd say, 'Oh wow, my mother's sunbeams!'"

At their dining table on the first day of the cruise, Pat and Ingrid met Sharon Lair, from Alameda, San Francisco's bay area, California. Sharon's sister, Cindy Flores, had passed away in 2009 and left Sharon enough money to take a cruise.

"My sister loved cruises and we never could afford to go on one," says Sharon. "I thought it would be a wonderful way to remember her, and also fulfill my dream of going on a Sylvia Browne cruise. When I met Ingrid and Pat, I kept thinking of my sister – we just hit it off like we'd known each other forever – like we were sisters, too."

Pat, Ingrid and Sharon

Sharon and her husband, Jim, are in sync when it comes to psychic phenomenon. "My husband is quite certain – and Sylvia Browne confirmed it – that he lived through the Civil War and died in it. In fact, he's lived and died in two previous wars and he encourages me to learn as much as I can." Sharon has studied astrology and numerology for thirty years, and has always sensed that she had intuitive abilities. She felt a true kinship with Ingrid and Pat.

"I feel very blessed to have met Ingrid in 2010," said Sharon, when she learned that Ingrid was having a book written about her life. "Meeting her was one of those rare and precious serendipitous 'instant' recognition moments. Although we've seen each other only a few times since that first cruise, we enjoy the shared deep sense of wonder and awe at the many gifts we all receive each and every day. Ingrid and I both have great husbands who love us for who we are and encourage our deeper spiritual exploration, even if they don't always understand it. And like Ingrid, I too had a difficult childhood and first marriage, so I've learned to appreciate, cherish and recognize unconditional love when it's offered."

Spiritual development and cruising on the high seas with new friends like Pat and Sharon was especially meaningful for Ingrid, as she felt herself growing in so many important ways. Just being on the ocean was already a comforting and mystical experience for Ingrid. Sunrise and sunset on board ship has always been magical for her.

"My favorite color is when the sky is peach and blue, either on sunrise or sunset – those same colors can be seen," she observes. "To me, it's the most beautiful sight in the world – even more beautiful than meteor showers."

For Ingrid and Pat, that first cruise together was fast and exciting. "We were both really interested in the intuitives and their messages," says Ingrid, explaining that her beliefs were reinforced and strengthened with each psychic cruise and workshop she took.

It has long been Ingrid's belief that we all have a sixth sense that is not developed. "We are born with it, but we don't work on it. It's been said that we use just a fraction of our brain and I believe that's so true. I doubt that you can ever achieve 100% of your brain capacity until you go home (heaven or the other side). We are in a bodily container on the earth until then, and when we go to the other side, we are more spiritual energy than body, but we do have a form and nearly everyone is about thirty years old chronologically – each of us with pure knowledge and no pain or hunger or weariness. Our energy never dies."

She truly hears the music of the mountain and the valley, the boulders and the bushes, the ocean and the dolphins singing.

Ingrid sees nearly tangible auras around people – beautiful, unique colors unlike any that are charted. It depends on their mood, she says, and their energy, as to what color their aura will be.

"I thought everybody saw auras," says Ingrid. "I've seen them since I was a child, but when I pointed it out, people gave me strange looks and I said to myself, 'uh oh,' and I kept silent after that."

She quotes one of her favorite philosophers, "Uncle Albert" (Albert Einstein): *"There are two ways to live. You can live as if nothing is a miracle or as if everything is a miracle."*

Living life as if everything is a miracle … Ingrid aspires to do that and usually succeeds. On her visit to Ponte Vedra Beach, Florida in 2011, Ingrid actually sat on Uncle Albert's lap at the home of her new friend, Sherry Chait! The Art Deco chair delighted her, and Uncle Albert obviously enjoyed meeting Ingrid, too!

Ingrid writes automatically. She's found it to be a miraculous way of communicating with her inner being as well as those spirits that have gone on to the other side. Often, she will experience the miracle of automatic writing at a time when all is calm and the night sky sparkles with stars over her mountain. It is a ritual that is somewhat like speaking in tongues, except that it happens with pen and paper. Sometimes, the automatic writing is actually a sketch of a place she is envisioning, such as the night she sketched jagged cliffs and trees and water surrounding an area in France where a plateau juts out and where Ingrid's mind/soul/spirit instructed her to write the words that Mary Magdalene is buried there. Also on that same paper, she scribbled references to names of the four children of Jesus and Mary.

"I do not know what I am writing," says Ingrid. "I try to understand it later. I want to have more time in my life to do this and understand it."

Ingrid believes she has evolved into a Christian Gnostic with deeper understanding than she has ever had before. "People say that Gnostics don't believe in God, but they are wrong. I totally believe in Father God and Mother God and in our brother Jesus and all the angels."

In one session with Sylvia, Ingrid remembers asking her about the three little monk-type people who were hanging around her dreams at night and scaring the living daylights out of her. She would see them when she meditated, and it seemed they were always at her bedside. They were little faceless, chubby ones with brown cloaks.

"I can't see their faces," she told Sylvia, "I want them to go away." Sylvia told her she wasn't dreaming. She said that they were the council and they were harmless, but if they bothered her, they would go away. And go away they did – just like that.

With or without the council present, Ingrid and Pat turned out to be perfect room-mates.

"If she wanted to sleep in, she could. If I wanted to go early, I could," recalls Ingrid. "Pat liked to order breakfast in the room and I thought that was great. She knew just what I wanted to eat, too. I usually had fruit and green tea and a blue-berry muffin – mostly vegetarian, staying away from meat." Pat's birthday cruise with Ingrid was the beginning of several psychic adventures the two soul sisters would experience together. It was a fabulous, mind-enhancing cruise for each of them, but there was still one missing ingredient – Ingrid's painting, *Crystal of Enchantment,* was not featured in the art auction on board the Holland America ship, nor were any other Jo Wall paintings.

"Ingrid went on her third cruise, and the painting still wasn't there," Pat told Jo. "Isn't there anything you can do to get that painting to her?"

Late in the fall of 2009, Ingrid dropped by her little post office in Homeland, California and there, waiting for her, was a large package from England! Jo had gone down into her basement at Wisteria Cottage, found an unsigned, unnumbered print of *Crystal of Enchantment*, and sent it to Ingrid along with a personal, handwritten note, and the lyrical words that accompany that painting, as follows:

Crystal of Enchantment
With her powerful crystal, the enchantress conjures spell-binding magic. Gramophone horns transform into morning glories pouring forth heavenly melodies and great ships sail from seashells to a land where fairies play. The whole world is radiant with magical light and all-encompassing love that flows from her powerful spirit.

Those treasures – the painting, the description and the hand-written letter from Josephine Wall, are now framed and hanging in a place of honor in Ingrid's living room.

"People always say the lady in the painting looks like me," says Ingrid, "but even more amazing than that is the fact that the artist is named Josephine – my mother's name.

"Josephine Wall is a beautiful spiritual person, the total opposite of my mom. It's like some kind of strange déjà vu that my favorite artist would bear the same name as my mother, who abused me so badly for so many years."

It was in March of 2010, in the mystical Red Rocks of Sedona, Arizona, that Ingrid had an opportunity to face the painful memories of her mother head-on when she attended a four-day Colette Baron-Reid Intensive at the Enchantment Resort in Sedona. There, Ingrid and Pat met up once again with their friend, Sharon Lair, and each of the women experienced some transformative moments that would help guide them on their future path.

Colette's creation called *The Goblin Method* helps identify and release any and all inner wounds that prevent success and drain your power. According to Colette, "The energies of this area (Sedona) are a portal to healing and accelerated awareness, making it the perfect setting to guide you through the process of reclaiming the wholeness that is within you."

In further describing *The Goblin Method*, Colette's website reads as follows:

"It's about releasing all false assumptions, and beliefs that you've learned about yourself and your relationship to the world around you. It's about removing all the blocks between you and the authentic YOU.

"Liberate 'The One Who Knows,' through the Goblin Method – a unique process of transformative self revelation. This method is specifically designed to transform fear into freedom, separation into unity, failure into success. An authentic life is led with courage and the knowledge of your unique purpose on earth. Discover your destiny when you liberate 'The One Who Knows,' the ancient wisdom keeper within you, as you identify your inner goblins of self-sabotage that represent the unconscious patterning that prevents your full potential."

Attendees at the four-day event were requested to bring comfortable clothing and shoes and attire suitable for hiking, as they would partake in a sacred ceremony and take a journey into the "Garden of Forgiveness" process at a Buddhist Stupa as well as participating in setting the intention for energetic integration at one of the seven vortexes in Sedona – the vortex of the universe. It was guaranteed that the magical intensive would shift lives and expand the capacity of participants to live in the "amazing Truth of who you are."

Ingrid's unique perspective on the experience is somewhat less mystical. "Colette created the goblin thing to help people get rid of the goblins in their lives. There was one lady at the intensive whose father always told her she would never amount to anything, she was good for nothing. He drove it into her constantly and as a result, she walked around with her shoulders down – no self-esteem at all. This intensive helps you get rid of those kinds of goblins."

One of the exercises, as described by Ingrid, is as follows: "There are three chairs. In the first chair, you tell what's bothering you, in the second chair, you're the goblin, and in the third chair, you're the lady who knows all and you talk to the goblin. 'What are you doing to Ingrid?' 'Ingrid, where do you want to leave those goblins?'" Ingrid laughs.

"I told the lady who knows all that I wanted to leave the goblins home with Richard because he's so analytical and strong!"

Basically, when using the Goblin Method, Ingrid was advised to make the goblin go and collect the bones of her childhood and throw them in the ocean depths and forget about them.

"Colette teases me that I'm getting younger and younger and pretty soon I'll be a little child – finally living the life I wanted to live as a child now – dancing and singing and blowing bubbles – living the life I was never allowed to live when I was a child."

In addition to the Goblin Method, there was a great deal of quiet meditation involved in the intensive.

"A lot of the time we couldn't talk," says Ingrid. "It was very introspective. There were times when we couldn't talk for the whole morning, and we each stayed alone in our own little casita at night. In the mornings, we had breakfast together, but there was much silence and peace. We placed stones around a Buddhist statue and walked around it seven times, asking for more compassion and peace on earth – everyone had a rose to give as an offering. There was a high, spiritual feeling the whole time."

On a less formal note, during what Ingrid terms "the goblin thing," it seemed that she attracted animals wherever she went, just as she always has done. There were the beautiful mountain quail that walked right up to her and the small herd of deer that followed her and peered into the window of the hall where they were meditating.

"Pat got all excited and pointed at the deer," laughs Ingrid, impishly adding, "I had to remind her not to be disturbing the goblin thing."

As Sharon participated in the four-day intensive experience along with Pat and Ingrid, she became even more aware of Ingrid's intuitive abilities, and Ingrid developed a special place in her heart for Sharon.

"Sharon is a great new friend," says Ingrid, "and I know that her husband, Jim, will get along so well with Richard. They are both quiet and very understanding of their 'woo-woo wives.'"

Jim, like Richard, stays behind while his wife explores the outer limits, although Jim is more amenable to cruising than Richard is. The older Richard gets, Ingrid notes, the more concerned he is for the little animals that depend on him for care. "When I get home from a cruise, I can tell that Richard's little kittens are safe and happy and grateful to have him," says Ingrid.

"She talks to animals so naturally," declares Sharon, remembering the animals at Sedona that seemed to follow Ingrid wherever she ventured.

"It's amazing to me. She's almost like an angel – not of this earth. She communicates with every living thing on the same level, and how she has gotten beyond the things that happened to her when she was young is a mystery to me. There's certainly nothing but love coming from her now – in every direction."

Sharon is excited about Ingrid's plan to open a healing and meditation center on her mountain. "I've seen Ingrid touch people and literally make them feel better," she says. "She did it to me. My ankle was hurting and it felt better the minute she touched it. I can't wait to go to her place on the mountain and meditate and learn in a beautiful setting!"

Speaking of Ingrid's plans to decorate her center with Josephine Wall's art, Sharon, too, has become a Jo Wall fan. "I bought Jo Wall's astrology cards and a mouse-pad," she says. "I'm a Cancer."

While in Sedona, each of the participants received a gift bag that included a Josephine Wall Journal, a CD of music from NASA, "with awesome sun sounds," and some of Colette's music, bath crystals, a bottle of soothing lavender oil and a little terra cotta jar with a tiny animal and a stone inside. "In the evening," Ingrid remembers, "we were to take a salt bath with the crystals and just lay there and allow the stress to escape, and then put on the oil (mine was the only bag that didn't have the oil in it) and play the CD and drift off to sleep with the terra cotta jar next to the bed. The little animal in mine was a sea turtle. We were supposed to write our dreams in the journal."

One night Ingrid dreamt there were three huge female angels in her room – thirty feet tall with beautiful white wings, each wearing a white gown with a golden rope belt.

Another night, she dreamed that there was a young couple in her room with their little girl and they had no place to stay that night. "They weren't supposed to be there, but they wanted to give me $20 to stay there and I was arguing with them, saying you really can't stay here," recalls Ingrid. "When I woke up, I felt so bad for them."

Strangely, that dream was a portent of things to come. Ingrid remembered the dream of the young couple and their child vividly the following summer when she and Richard purchased a home in Marietta, California for Heidi and her family to live in.

"It's in a beautiful area, close to the freeway, yet in a really nice tract – an older 1990 two-story home surrounded by beautiful parks and nice schools, right around the corner from the Mormon church," says Ingrid. "It looks like a wonderful neighborhood for Preston True to grow up in, and I feel as good about that home as I felt bad about that poor couple with the little girl in my dream."

Back to those "Woo Woo Cruises," Ingrid and Pat were room-mates again on a Sylvia Browne psychic cruise in 2010 that embarked from Cape Canaveral, Florida. This time, Pat asked Ingrid to fly in a day early and spend the night at Pat's home, which is also Florida's most complete gallery of original Josephine Wall art.

"I loved Pat's house! The Josephine Wall paintings are astounding and they were all over the place. Pat's house was full of fairies and fantasy and it was delightful to me," declares Ingrid, describing her own home as "mostly office – cluttered with paper work everywhere."

It was in May, soon after she returned from the cruise swimming with the dolphins in Bimini, Bahamas, that Ingrid attended a Hay House "I Can Do It" Conference in San Diego and learned what her next adventure would be.

"I pulled the Colette card to see what this was going to be all about, thinking to myself that I would find out what I was supposed to do at this conference. I found out alright! About fifty people at that conference told me I needed to write a book about my life. Even in the elevator, people who didn't even know me told me I was destined to write a book about my life. It was meant to be, and somehow, I knew that Pat Sager and Josephine Wall would be involved in the book and in the rest of my life."

Since meeting the art of Josephine Wall on a cruise ship, in a nutrition store, and again in the home of Pat Sager, the walls of Ingrid's living room have become an art gallery of sorts, as well. Seven of Jo Wall's paintings (three of them originals) are hung in Ingrid's living room, and the best part is that Richard also loves the art of Josephine Wall. In June of 2010, when Pat visited their mountain home, she brought with her a special gift for Richard – a lithograph of *The Millenium Tree* (or Tree of Peace) painted by Jo Wall. Her thinking was that Richard would enjoy the scientific aspect of the painting, which he definitely did.

In the one little office room where Ingrid does most of her "Extreme Work", she is surrounded by the dolls and toys she never had as a child.

"It's like a little girl's room. I have dolls and musical toys that sing and dance, all sorts of musical toys that delight me." Ingrid admits that her home is somewhat bizarre in that she and Richard are both collectors and don't mind clutter. Richard collects tiny model cars and those fill every spare space that is not taken up with other collectibles that both of them enjoy.

Richard adores Ingrid and misses her when she is gone. Although she limits her trips to seven days at a time, her pursuit of psychic experiences continues to expand and takes her away more and more frequently.

"I'm enjoying this new freedom and awareness – exploring my inner being through cruising and swimming with dolphins and attending intensives in Sedona – it's all been an incredible experience except that it involves leaving Richard all by himself because he refuses to leave the mountain. Part of me always stays home with him and no matter how lovely the trip, part of me can't wait to get back to him. That's why I want to establish my own healing center nearby. I'm a healer – a shaman – and even though Richard and I don't talk about it right now, my Circle of Love Healing Center will be established here on our own mountain someday. It is my destiny."

Chapter 11

Inside the Circle of Love

There was a moment in time, at eight years old, when Ingrid felt so sad, so hopeless and unloved, that suicide seemed the only way out.

"I climbed that elm tree in our backyard and let myself fall off the tallest branch because I wanted to die," she remembers. "God had other plans for me, though. He knew I'd grow from outcast to member of the inner circle of love. He knew that my destiny was to bring others into the circle of love, as well."

Wherever she travels, Ingrid gathers people into her ever-widening circle. Last Thanksgiving, as she waited at the Dallas/Fort Worth Airport on her way to Virginia, she saw a young family of four seated nearby. Ingrid watched, smiling, as the little boy and girl, ages about two and three, stood with their noses pinned against the big window looking out at the airplanes. Once in a while, one or both of the children – eyes popping with wonder – sweet voices filled with excitement - would dash back to their parents to point to something of interest out on the tarmac.

Sitting next to Ingrid was a woman in her sixties, who glanced up occasionally from the newspaper she read.

"I hope I don't have to sit near those children," she confided grimly to Ingrid, her loud, nasal New York accent carrying far enough to merit a worried glance from the young parents. Ingrid was aghast.

"Oh my gosh!" she declared, with a wary smile. "Don't you remember when you were a child? What would love do?"

Still smiling hopefully at the woman, Ingrid said gently, "They are such beautiful, well-behaved children. I would love to sit by them!"

Looking back on that airport encounter, Ingrid feels that is exactly what she is supposed to be doing with her life – reaching out to hurting people with healing love, one person at a time.

"That woman's whole attitude changed after I said what I said to her," she recalls. "She suddenly became very friendly and nice. The young parents were beaming. The little ones never even noticed … they were too busy watching the airplanes."

It was just one short moment in time, but because of Ingrid's healing spirit, several people were drawn into her circle of love that day at the airport.

There have been many times like that for Ingrid – times when she was waiting in line or working as a server or simply in a room full of people.

"When you think you're having a bad day, there's always someone else that needs more cheering up than you do," says Ingrid. "The day is what you make it. No matter what, I try to make it a good day."

Since that first psychic cruise back in 2007, Ingrid has had more good days than ever before. Inspired by what she is

learning and doing, she senses that she is supposed to be taking these frequent trips to explore intuitiveness; to learn more about her close connection with healing, and to bond with the hearts and spirits of other people of like mind. Ingrid knows that she is being groomed to learn more, and know more, so that she can eventually do more.

Already, the innate power of healing that shc has always sensed within her is getting stronger and more focused.

Early in 2010, when Ingrid attended a family wedding in Hawaii, she found that her sister Enid was still quite ill with cancer of the larynx and she renewed her efforts to promote healing. While performing her healing ritual with Enid this time, all the while insisting that she continue with the medical treatments prescribed by doctors, Ingrid and Enid were both profoundly affected. Enid felt an immediate sense of well-being and Ingrid grew uncomfortably warm with the effort and became totally drained of energy, to the point that she was so exhausted upon returning to California that she was weak and listless for several days.

"Enid's cancer was advanced. I think that is why the healing exhausted me so much," says Ingrid. "Now the doctors don't see any sign of her cancer. None. She is cancer-free. She still has to do the radiation to make sure they got it all, but they think it's gone."

Enid's doctor, Judy L. Schmidt, M.D. of the Maui Medical Group, Inc. (Hematology/Oncology), is amazed at her patient's prognosis. "Enid is magic to me," said Dr. Schmidt, who is in complete agreement that there are those, like Ingrid, who have healing powers that can greatly enhance recovery.

To her sister's delight, Enid's speech began improving and she began feeling so well that she started making plans to go on a cruise in 2011 through the Panama Canal with her family," exclaims Ingrid. "It's thrilling to hear her making plans for a full and happy future!"

Speaking of full and happy futures, it was on September 12, 2010 that Ingrid and Richard's oldest grandson, Jesse Reeves, married his sweetheart, Brittney, in an unusual wedding ceremony on a large, cleared portion of their mountain property fondly called "the ball park."

"The ball park is where we've always played family ball games, ever since we first moved out here over thirty years ago," Ingrid recalls. "It has sentimental meaning to Jesse and to his dad, Jason, too. I'm so glad they chose to have their wedding ceremony there. Richard spent several days clearing the land for the wedding and it was well worth it, as the tent went up and a beautiful white horse-drawn carriage came to carry the lovely bride and her handsome groom to a joyful future together."

Jesse has always had a special place in Ingrid's heart, not only because he was the first grandchild, but because he shares her birthday – January 24th. As a Navy submariner, young Jesse is receiving the same kind of excellent training that prepared his father, Jason, to come into the family business nearly twenty years ago. Ingrid and Richard look forward to Jesse doing the same when he leaves the Navy; returning to California to become an integral part of Reeves & Woodland Industries, the successful family business that his grandparents built.

"In a little over a year from his wedding date, Jesse will be working with his dad and the company will be as Richard and I envisioned it so long ago – a family business that goes on and on through the generations," says Ingrid. "As we step back and they step forward, the extreme work will finally be behind Richard and me."

A woman whose life has been filled with extreme work, extreme pain and extreme joy, Ingrid prefers to dwell on the joyful aspects, such as reminiscing with Richard about the four children they raised together at the Triple R Ranch.

One day as they sat on a high boulder looking out on their property and reminiscing, Richard and Ingrid came up with the following insights on their four:

"Wayne, the oldest, was the most determined boy I've ever known. He still is that way," said Richard. "When he decided to be a guitar player, he played until his fingers were blistered and bloody and calloused. It didn't matter to him that his hands were swollen and sore – he played many hours a day every day until he perfected it. He eventually switched from Jimmy Hendrix to religion – now he plays and writes strictly gospel – but whatever Wayne does, he does it to the fullest and he masters it completely. He did the same thing with welding, and became an expert at TIG welding [a form of welding which takes an exacting hand and a lot of patience]. Wayne always applies himself 100%."

Richard and Ingrid point to Jason as the winner of any family game that involved engineering or mechanics. "He was always great with mechanics," says Ingrid. Richard adds, "Jason came out of the Navy as a qualified nuclear operator of submarines and went right to work for the company. After his training in the Navy, especially with his natural engineering ability, he was perfectly equipped to work with the conventional power plants that our company deals with. He also rebuilds Mustangs better than new. Jason is a genius when it comes to mechanical engineering of any kind. He's always been the top mechanic of the family. He's the only one of the four that has stayed with the company and worked side by side with Ingrid and me for twenty years."

Ingrid notes that Jason has always been the most honest of the four – the one that would confess, no matter how badly the truth hurt. She also fondly remembers rocket days on the mountain, when the kids would carve the yucca plants into rockets and place little engines in them and Jason's rocket always went the fastest and highest, hands down.

Chris was also a top mechanic as a teenager, and enjoyed restoring cars and working on engines, but he was more a biker and a jock than a mechanic, according to his dad. "He was always going out and developing his body – mountain biking and hiking. Chris is the Grizzly Adams of the family."

Richard talks proudly of the cabin that Chris and his sons have built way up in the mountains of Colorado. "You take your life in your hands just going up there in the winter," said Richard, noting that the elevation is 10,400 feet and it is total wilderness, but Chris thrives on it. Chris also works with Reeves & Woodland Industries on occasion as a private contractor.

Ingrid calls Chris a great storyteller and a good writer. According to Ingrid, Chris and Heidi could come up with some stories that were whoppers, especially after Richard taught them to play Liar's Poker.*

*Liar's Poker is played with a deck of regular playing cards. Everybody draws one card without looking at it and holds it – face outward – on their forehead. The other players know what everybody else has, but no one knows what their own card is. With everyone laughing and pointing, the bets go around – some people dropping out – some people raising their bets. The object is to make people think they have nothing – especially if they happen to have an ace! The best liars are usually the winners.

"Richard could kick himself today because he taught them to play that game," says Ingrid. "We used to play it a lot, but one day we found out that Heidi and Chris had lied straight-faced to the people at school and then ditched school for the day. We turned them in ourselves and made sure they were punished so that they knew how serious it was. After that, though, no more Liars Poker was played at the Triple R Ranch!"

When Ingrid talks of her daughter, Heidi, a tender smile can be heard in her voice. "Heidi was a beautiful, caring, loving child and, today, she is a wonderful mother to her son. She's the daughter I always wanted. In my younger years, I made this decoupage picture for Heidi that said, "I made a wish and Heidi came true."

Looking back, Richard remembers Heidi as the most gifted of the four children. "Heidi was probably more intelligent than the rest of them combined," said Richard. "She always seemed to be one step ahead of them – and she didn't have to study. If Heidi wanted to do it, she could do it. She was the smart one of the bunch."

Looking back at those days when they first moved out to the mountain and lived like pioneers without electricity, Richard and Ingrid agree that their four kids have turned out quite well.

"We made them all do their homework every day," says Richard. "And each of them had old-time farm chores to accomplish, too. We had twenty-one acres and rabbits and chickens – even had pigs at one time. Ask Ingrid about the pigs … she had them well-trained!"

Laughing, Ingrid chimes in. "We had two pigs," she says, "I named them Das Limpet (from a German cartoon) and Norman. I did have them well-trained. I'd tell them to roll over and I'd scratch their bellies with a stick. I always told the kids not to make pets of the animals because they were going to be for dinner, but that didn't apply to my pigs. I never liked pork much, anyway. Both of those pigs lived to die of old age!"

Speaking of old age, neither Richard nor Ingrid are on that plateau, despite the fact that they have reached their mid-sixties at the time of this writing. They are an attractive, youthful-looking couple with a healthy glow about them and an aura of friendly companionship that is evident in the comfortable way they lean toward one another to pose for photographs.

In a photograph taken on September 12th 2010 at the wedding of Jesse and Brittney, Ingrid is stunning in a beautiful blue swirling scarf-like chiffon two-piece dress with golden sandals on her pretty feet while Richard looks handsome in his tan cap and slacks with a cool, brightly colored race-car shirt. Behind them, the sun glints golden on the high boulders of a craggy mountain peak.

Richard and Ingrid on their mountain

"That's our mountain," says Ingrid, proudly standing next to her man on the land they have worked so diligently to preserve.

It is the picture of a successful couple who are comfortable in their skin – pleased with who they are and where they have arrived in life.

"Ingrid is and always has been the nucleus of our family," says Richard, "and, for thirty years, she was the foundation and cornerstone of our business. She is the heart of us – very much in the center of our circle, surrounded by love."

As to the "woo-woo stuff" that so fascinates his beloved wife of thirty-three years, Richard is tolerant of Ingrid's exploration. He accepts her quest and is still somewhat mystified about the whole thing.

"I'm not into it myself," he says, "but if you're not sure about what's right or wrong, then you'd better be kind of careful before you criticize. I know that our science is advancing every day. We have a great history of advancing science in the last century, and the truth is that, mathematically, who knows whether there are other universes. Ingrid is quite talented and unique. She's always had a wonderful outlook on life – who knows what is far out and what isn't?"

Who knows?

For Ingrid Reeves, nearly every moment of life is far out and far away from the dark memories of her childhood. Each moment, in fact, sparkles like mountain sunshine on the iridescent glow of a tiny hummingbird. Her constant smile lights up a room and her light-hearted laugh is a welcome diversion from the ordinary. Eagerly, she embraces life with no signs of slowing down. She dances whenever the music plays, she digs her toes in the sandy beach whenever the opportunity presents itself, and she takes off into the air to travel far and near for psychic seminars and enriching educational experiences.

Diving into the surf and swimming with the dolphins is a pure delight for her. Standing on the bow of the boat and blowing bubbles out to the universe is a pastime she treasures. Searching the night sky for meteor showers is a regular pursuit.

Ingrid savors life. She is thrilled to meet people and innocently expects (and almost always receives) the best that each person has to offer. Today, she is, indeed, far out. Far out from the sad little girl who sought to end her life so many years ago and closer than ever to the happy child within her. Ingrid is actually reliving the childhood of her dreams today – skipping, not scrubbing; laughing, not crying; playing, not working.

"I'm living backwards in my fantasy room of Josephine Wall art," she chimes. "I look around me and I see beauty everywhere I look. Even that gorgeous aqua dress I wore to Brittney's wedding is part of the fantasy. It was a fairy dress of soft, flowing material that made me feel like a goddess."

And a goddess she is … the blonde goddess of the magic mountain retreat that she and Richard have spent thirty years carving out of the wilderness.

"I love you," she tells Richard when she returns from one of her psychic sojourns on the sea.

"I love you more," he replies.

Together, they ride to the top of their mountain in the Jeep. Holding hands, they climb up on the boulders and survey their property, enjoying the satisfaction that comes from a job well-done. It has been more than three decades since they first sat on a boulder and watched in fascination as a mountain lion and her cubs roamed freely on the pristine land. Today, although they have laboriously worked to preserve their own beautiful spot of green in the mountain valley, most of their property remains as unspoiled as it was the day they first laid eyes on it.

While Ingrid explores psychic phenomenon from one end of the globe to the other, Richard remains at home on their mountain or what he calls "the farm," and takes care of the animals. There are five cats who receive his devoted love and protection daily – Missy M is a tiger cat with the letter M emblazoned on her forehead ("one of those Maryland cats," says Ingrid). Mister Gray has long gray hair that surrounds his face like the mane of a lion. Mama Cat and her two kittens (who are growing fast) have been especially privileged in that Richard has set aside one of his glassed-in conservatories to protect them from coyotes.

"They all came from Habib, one of Jason's cats that came to live with us. She looked Egyptian – just beautiful – and, sadly, she was killed by an owl," says Ingrid. "Coyotes aren't the only predators out here on our mountain – there are the owls and huge redwing hawks that swoop in and prey on little kittens and cats."

One of the two swiftly growing kittens is fondly named "Dustball" because she is always rolling in the dirt,

and the other is "Tripper" – a kitten who gets underfoot and trips up its two-legged caretakers often. They are Richard's little charges and he takes wonderful care of them.

"Richard and I have always taken care of our animals, including the hummingbirds that hover all around here. We've made sure the cats don't climb up after them when they're nesting in the tall pine trees," says Ingrid. In the spring of 2011, she counted and said, "Right now, we have four hummingbird nests with two babies in each nest, and Richard is as intent on keeping them safe as he is in keeping the cats safe."

Once, about three years ago, Richard and Ingrid saw two hummingbirds ganging up on another hummingbird. "They were using their long beaks like little swords," recalls Ingrid. "They were viciously stabbing the poor little bird and it had fallen to the ground, nearly dead. I'm pretty sure they were males, claiming their territory. I've learned that hummingbirds are quite territorial." Richard and Ingrid could not bear to see the tiny hummingbird die. "We shooed the two away, and I picked up the little bird and spoke healing words to it as we put it in a cardboard box and took it to the back forty of our property. I told him [the hummingbird] … 'now you have your own territory.'"

It wasn't until Ingrid's dramatic rescue of the tiny hummingbird in Costa Rica in 2011 that she recognized her muse. It has always been the hummingbird – a colorful, jewel-like "air-dancer" that darted happily in and out of her life, enhancing the music and the beauty. It has been said that hummingbirds fly on iridescent wings of glittering gauze, free of time, representing hope, love and beauty. Ingrid, with her brilliant manner of dress, her boundless energy, and her sparkling smile, is much like the hummingbird. It's nearly impossible to hold back the smile that comes when you spot a hummingbird or when you lay eyes on Ingrid … the pure spirit of each inspires instant joy.

In her book *The Map*, Colette Baron-Reid describes serendipity as a gift that is bestowed upon "the curious and openhearted." Ingrid, with her pure, openhearted spirit, has received a bonus share of serendipity since turning age sixty and began her journey toward spiritual awakening.

"Serendipity is bestowed upon the curious and openhearted, and reminds you again that what happens on the journey is a magical unseen arrangement of potentials and possibilities," writes Colette. Serendipity was working overtime when Ingrid's tiny muse became trapped on the ceiling of a magical resort in Costa Rica, nearly repeating one of the most dramatic moments of Ingrid's childhood. As always, when one of God's creatures was hurt, Ingrid rushed to lay on her healing hands. This time, as never before, Ingrid and the object of her healing became one. "I am the hummingbird," she declares, laughing at serendipitous discovery of that rich, beautiful oneness that has always been there.

Hummingbirds and hard hats … Ingrid's life has been a fascinating mix of laughter and tears, freedom and slavery, happiness and hard work – and, like the hummingbird, she has remained undaunted by the elements and fiercely protective of her territory, family and personality. Curious and openhearted she is, indeed, and beneath that soft, beautiful, childlike persona is a strong, courageous, hardworking pioneer woman – a woman whose pure, healing spirit can move mountains.

Sunshine, bubbles and happiness are her goals for her Circle of Love mountain meditation center, if it is meant to be. "The place is not as important as the mission," says Ingrid,

noting that her recent travels have taken her to so many areas of the world where healing is taking place and bubbles of happiness abound. Bubbles, with their rainbow of translucent colors, have so often floated on the mountain breezes during the past three decades, adding delightful sparkling moments to the hard work of living. Appreciating the simple pleasures of life, Ingrid, Richard and their children – especially Ingrid – delighted in blowing bubbles and watching them drift toward the boulders and blue skies of their mountain sanctuary.

Today, there are "bubbles" of a different color on Reeves' mountain – in the form of fabulous copper bubble domes built by Richard, whose lifelong interest in astronomy has come to fruition with prosperity and approaching retirement. Richard, always the inventor and explorer, has built a couple of domed star-gazing observatories of the most advanced sort. There, he studies astronomy to his heart's content while Ingrid studies her healing and intuitive arts. As she learns, she grows in the desire to share her newfound knowledge with others at a meditation center where inner healing and spiritual renewal can take place.

She envisions what such a center will look like.

"It will be awesome to build a wonderful fairy cottage-like center where there would be a large gallery with Josephine Wall paintings and another huge room that is a library and sitting area with a fireplace … big quiet rooms just for sitting and meditating. There will be little casitas surrounding the main cottage where families can bond and mend their differences and grow closer together in the circle of love."

Just as Richard used to lead the "Fagawee Tribe" on hikes up the mountain, Ingrid hopes that the people who seek peace and family harmony at the Circle of Love Center will experience that same relationship with nature and with one

another. Love, bubbles and peace will flourish, with incredible vistas at every turn and the high-pitched music of hummingbirds in the trees and gardens of the sanctuary.

Because of the incredible heat during the summer months, she envisions a mountain meditation center as a seasonal place – possibly open only from October through June – but the healing will happen perpetually, wherever Ingrid is. There will be many moments when Ingrid and Richard will simply spend time together and enjoy their tranquil life on the mountain. For both of them, reflecting on the journey of life – past, present and future – is a daily exercise, and for Ingrid, exploration into the unknown and expectation of miracles and magic are on the agenda for the rest of her life.

By early 2011, her travel schedule had become mind-boggling. After a cruise to Mexico with psychic Lisa Williams in October of 2010, Ingrid traveled in November to Philadelphia to spend time with Pat Sager and her fiancé, G. B. Lane, as well as to finally meet U.K. artist Josephine Wall and her husband Bob.

Josephine was booked through Kirks Folly to appear on their QVC Television Show and Ingrid experienced the fun of being on the set and seeing the production up close, as well as having some time to visit intimately with her favorite artist.

"I was so honored," recalls Ingrid. "Josephine and Bob and I had breakfast together for several mornings, and at one two-hour session, Josephine sat at a computer and showed me her entire website, describing the meaning behind some of her paintings and even her painting process. She's an amazing artist and a beautiful person."

In January 2011, Ingrid traveled to Jacksonville, Florida for a brief stay with her biographer, Susan D. Brandenburg,

Bob and G.B. with Ingrid, Jo and Pat in Philly

where she attended a wrestling tournament at Ponte Vedra High School and loudly cheered on Susan's grandson, Drew Daniel, captain of the wrestling team (finding it oddly reminiscent of Richard's days of high school wrestling, long before he and Ingrid met). Ingrid was also the guest of honor at a special dinner party given by artist Susanne Schuenke, an internationally acclaimed painter who resides in Ponte Vedra Beach. At the spectacular Circle of Love Dinner Party, attended by a diverse and interesting group of twelve ladies, Susan did a small reading from this book – an excerpt that was nearly as well-received and applauded as the glittering guest of honor.

On the day following the elegant dinner party in Ponte Vedra Beach, Ingrid embarked on a Caribbean cruise with Hay House from Fort Lauderdale, followed by Colette Baron-Reid's psychic boot camp in Costa Rica.

Susanne Schuenke & Ingrid Reeves
Ponte Vedra Beach, FL
Circle of Love Dinner Party - January 2011

While in Costa Rica, important breakthroughs occurred for Ingrid. One, she magically met her muse face to face when she and Colette teamed up for the dramatic rescue of a tiny hummingbird. Two, when Ingrid walked into a little boutique run by two Turkish gypsies, she was instantly drawn to an ancient prayer stone amulet, a brilliant circle of red carnelian (about two inches in diameter) with hieroglyphics etched into it. Since bringing the beautiful gold-encircled medallion home, Ingrid has researched carnelians in a book written by her daughter-in-law Shirley Street entitled Heavenly Birthstones and Personalities. The carnelian is the Stone of Judah (the tribe of Jesus). The name comes from Latin, meaning raw flesh. It is also called the Martyr Stone – red like fire or blood. Like Jesus, the Lion of Judah and Ingrid's ultimate spirit guide, the carnelian represents the pure in heart. Genesis 49:8-12. For as far back as she can remember, Ingrid has envisioned a red ball of healing. Now, she holds a lovely symbol of that red ball next to her heart.

The Carnelian is but one more confirmation that God is directing her on her amazing journey.

Next, Ingrid attended the April 12, 2011 Camelot wedding in Las Vegas of Pat Sager and her fiancé, G.B. Lane, with Merlin the Magician performing the nuptials, and a fabulous reception for the wedding party planned a few days later at the Enchanted Manor, a Five Star B&B on the Isle of Wight in the U.K.

The Enchanted Manor, owned and operated by Ric and Maggie Hilton, is filled with the beautiful art of Josephine Wall. For Ingrid, having been enchanted originally by Jo Wall's fabulous painting, *Crystal of Enchantment*, with its butterflies, bubbles and hummingbirds, attending a magical wedding reception and re-enactment of a Jo Wall Painting at the Enchanted Manor was truly coming full circle.

As to what the future holds, Ingrid leaves that to the whims of the universe, placing it in the loving hands of God and all His angels. Now thoroughly enjoying every aspect of her charmed existence, Ingrid looks forward to a full and exciting life as she looks back on the dark days of her childhood to discern a distinct pattern in God's plan. The plan, she has discovered, included the unrelenting abuse she suffered at the hands of her troubled mother, Josephine Olivier Marcus.

"Even though she abused me horribly, my mother taught me about hard work, and that has helped me get where I am today," says Ingrid. "I loved her and feared her at the same time. It was always that way – from the first time I remember seeing her when I was five years old until the day she died, screaming from the pain of cancer and still looking at me with scorn in her eyes. I believe it is because of my mother that I can feel the pain in people and that I have the strength and resolve to help heal that pain. I learned early that I could do anything, because I had to do it or suffer greatly. That is Mums' legacy to me. I have had to heal my own pain all of my life, seeking out the beauty where I could find it. Now, I can use that strong healing spirit to help others."

Early Spanish explorers to Trinidad called the hummingbird *Joyas voladoras*, which means “flying jewel.”

With her extraordinary sparkle, joy and energy, Ingrid Reeves is truly a *Joyas voladoras*!

Ingrid has accepted the hummingbird as her personal totem (an Algonquin word used by anthropologists to define a symbol which possesses special wisdom for an individual, tribe, clan or family).

For those who believe in animal totems, the hummingbird is said to have its own special medicine to help its chosen human develop what is needed in life. Totem spirits make themselves known to their humans, and once known, they work their magic.

The Hummingbird Totem heals with laser light speed, endures hardship bravely, savors long journeys, and always brings joy, happiness and love to all within its circle.

Like the flying jewel that is her totem, Ingrid has learned to adapt to whatever life brings and to make the most of every difficult situation. She has learned to dance in the light, sing in the shadows, laugh in the darkness, and soar through the sunbeams. Hovering happily like the hummingbird she is, Ingrid enjoys the magic of being alive. She invites you to join her in the joyous journey.

Chapter 12

My Feathered Friends

Just as Ingrid saw herself in Josephine Wall's painting, *Crystal of Enchantment*, Stefanee Evans of Montpelier, Vermont saw herself in Jo's painting *My Feathered Friends*, the original of which was eventually purchased by Ingrid.

Upon their meeting in Las Vegas in April of 2011, Ingrid and Stefanee immediately recognized one another as kindred spirits ("feathered friends"). Following the renaissance wedding ceremony of Pat Sager and G. B. Lane at the Excalibur Hotel, performed by Merlin the Magician, the dancing wedding fairy (Stefanee) and the lovely Matron of Honor (Ingrid) whirled and twirled joyfully to the delight of the minstrels and onlookers as the costumed wedding party made its way to the banquet at the Camelot Steakhouse. Sharon Lair and her husband, Jim, were among the Lords and Ladies applauding and enjoying the two laughing "ladies of the dance."

Later, when traveling to the U.K. for Pat and G.B.'s dramatic wedding re-enactment of Jo Wall's painting, "The Enchanted Forest," Ingrid and Stefanee continued to cement a friendship that is destined to last a lifetime.

"Stefanee and I never stopped talking for the entire eight hour flight from Miami to Heathrow Airport," declares Ingrid. Actually, there was a brief break in their conversation that must be noted here by Ingrid's biographer, Susan D. Brandenburg.

I, Susan, was also a participant in Pat's global wedding, and a fellow passenger on the flight to Heathrow. The following is a description of what led up to and what followed that "brief break" in Ingrid and Stefanee's eight-hour conversation enroute to Heathrow:

The seating on the flight was arranged thusly: Susan sat in the aisle seat and next to her at the window was a lady named Elizabeth. Stefanee and Ingrid chattered away in the window and aisle seat behind Susan, with Pat and G.B. sleeping away in the seats behind them. Susan struck up a traveler-type "get-acquainted" conversation with Elizabeth, who revealed that she was giving herself a trip to Paris for her 42nd birthday. Elizabeth's husband had died of a heart attack in 2008. She confessed that she, too, had high blood pressure and that she hoped she wouldn't get dizzy on this flight as she had in the past. Elizabeth told Susan that she works as a security guard at Disneyworld in Orlando, Florida, and is currently in charge of Goofy and Ariel, but had at one time been in charge of Mickey and Minnie Mouse. She proudly showed Susan a photo of herself with Mickey and Minnie.

After dinner, as Susan became engrossed in a movie, Elizabeth tapped her arm, saying, "I'm dizzy." Her appearance was frightening. Her face was red, her breathing shallow, her skin hot as fire. Elizabeth appeared to be a perfect candidate for a stroke or heart attack. "What can I do for you?" asked Susan. "My blood pressure medication is in my checked luggage," gasped Elizabeth in response. Susan was in the process of buzzing the stewardess when she glimpsed Ingrid, laughing and talking with Stefanee behind her.

"Get up here right now, Ingrid!" ordered Susan, frantically pointing at Elizabeth. Words were unnecessary … Ingrid immediately sensed the woman's desperate straits. Grabbing Elizabeth's hand, she rushed her to the bulkhead where the stewardess sits for take-off and landing. The two of them sat on the narrow ledge-type seat with their heads together, holding hands and conversing quietly as the stewardess was apprised of Elizabeth's condition. By the time Pat found some baby aspirin for the dizzy woman and the stewardess brought oxygen to give to her, the emergency had passed. Ingrid had healed her. Coming back to her seat, Elizabeth seemed to have recovered completely from her dizzy spell. Later, she marveled at what had happened. "I don't know what your friend did to me," she confided to Susan, "but I haven't felt this good in years."

Soon, Ingrid and Stefanee were once again deep in their marathon conversation. When congratulated by the stewardess and others for her quick, healing action, Ingrid just shrugged and smiled. "It was probably a combination of my angels, some healing prayers and the human touch," she said modestly. Ingrid's bright smile, soft voice, pure loving spirit and healing human touch combined to make powerful medicine, indeed.

That powerful medicine has always been within her and continues to grow as she learns to control it. Time after time, Ingrid's pure loving spirit has shielded her personally as well as healing others. Much like the hardy little hummingbird that appears so delicate, yet survives the harshest elements, Ingrid's innocent, non-judgmental, friendly demeanor has the power to calm the storm and disarm the aggressor. With those rare exceptions over the years that have not responded to her kind, loving manner, Ingrid has learned that those aggressors must simply be endured, ignored and forgiven.

Ingrid has weathered those storms with grace and love … first in the form of her mother, and later, with those rare few who have failed to be touched by her loving spirit. In dealing with insensitive, unresponsive persons, Ingrid has instinctively followed the teachings of Jesus Christ. "Whoever does not receive you, nor heed your words, as you go out of that house or that city, shake the dust off your feet." [Matthew 10:13] By symbolically shaking the dust off her feet, Ingrid moves on with forgiveness in her heart, simply choosing to separate herself from those dark, negative influences and continue to seek the light.

Ingrid's ministry to fellow travelers didn't end until the last leg of her journey home from the wedding trip to the Isle of Wight. "I was at the Las Vegas Airport and there was a two-hour delay," she recalls. "The waiting area was jammed with people and I was really grateful to find a seat. I was sitting there reading when this man about my age stalked up to me and said, 'You need to move over! In fact, you need to get up and give me your seat!' I was a little stunned, but then I thought about it and I said, 'Okay.'"

Ingrid gathered her luggage and went over to an empty spot on the floor next to the wall, sitting there for the next hour and a half. "I was comfortable," she says, "and it was obvious that man needed to sit down. He needed the seat more than I did. That kind of thing happens to me all the time. No big deal."

So many lessons of life can be learned by simply using the gifts God has given to each of us. One of the gifts Ingrid has been given is generosity.

Josephine Wall, for instance, was gifted with the ability to create gorgeous images with her paintbrush. In the hearts of both Ingrid and Stefanee, Jo's painting *My Feathered Friends* touched a deep, primal knowing that they can now share with one another. When Stefanee first laid eyes on the painting in 2008, it was as if a window of new possibility opened for her. She was drawn into the beautiful scene, which helped her to communicate on a deeper level with her daughter, Angela.

Stefanee identified with the graceful goddess mounted on the flying horse, riding in a rainbow filled with feathered friends. Below the horse, a beautiful young girl soared in the air above a barren landscape, searching for love that was already in her heart, and seeking the rainbow of hope. Stefanee saw that the young girl's hands were clasped and her eyes closed, as if in prayer for the future that awaited her beyond the canvas.

Remembering the powerful impact of that painting on their lives, Stefanee declares, "One day, my daughter will share my vision for the world and make it a better place than I ever can. This painting of *My Feathered Friends* is truly about us."

Ingrid, who later purchased the original painting, also feels a kinship to the goddess on the flying horse, and the young girl soaring below. "That's me up there, and my daughter, Heidi, who is still seriously seeking answers on a barren landscape," says Ingrid. "I feel it is my destiny to provide a sanctuary for her and for others – a place where answers can be discovered and wounds healed. Until I met Stefanee, I envisioned a meditation center on my mountain. Now, I have the feeling that it may end up in Stefanee's magical forest in Vermont."

Wherever the meditation center turns out to be, it became clear in April of 2011 that Ingrid and Stefanee were slated to work together to make the world a better place.

The fates have been working overtime in preparing the path on which Ingrid and Stefanee now walk. In 2009, when she purchased *My Feathered Friends,* Ingrid had not yet recognized her muse, the hummingbird.

"I knew that the painting had deep meaning in my life, just as Jo's "Crystal of Enchantment" did," says Ingrid, "But it wasn't until Colette and I rescued the hummingbird in Costa Rica that it all began to make sense to me about *My Feathered Friends* – I've truly been a hummingbird from the very beginning and didn't know it. Even the place of my birth was a clue to the way my life would turn out!"

Trinidad, where Ingrid was conceived and born, is known as "The land of the hummingbird." Ingrid's hummingbird can be seen on the nation's coat of arms:

The late Chilean Poet Pablo Neruda was famous for writing beautiful love poems. His love poem, *Ode to the Hum-*

mingbird, could have been written about Ingrid. Neruda called the hummingbird a "water-spark, an incandescent drip of American fire," so aptly describing Ingrid's glitter and energy that it is almost as if he had the pleasure of meeting her. In another passage of the same poem, Neruda talks of the stout-heartedness of the hummingbird and how the falcon's black plumage does not daunt her. "You pirouette, a light within a light …" he wrote, again describing the brave little girl who scrubbed floors and dreamed of dancing with handsome princes in elegant ballrooms, learning to be undaunted by the darkness of life and the cruelty of her mother; to dance in the face of scorn and light up the room with her constant smile.

In Poole, Dorset, England, Ingrid, Stefanee and Susan had the great thrill of visiting the fabulous Art Gallery of

L-R Ingrid, author Susan D. Brandenburg, artist Josephine Wall, and Stefanee

Josephine Wall. Even more touching was the invitation from the artist and her husband, Bob Coulson, to spend the night at their charming home, Wisteria Cottage. Having written Jo's biography, *Palette of Dreams*, Susan was especially excited to see her words springing to life in the gorgeous garden and the hand-carved wooden stairway leading to the attic studio where Josephine's canvases are transformed into masterpieces. There, in the guestroom where Susan slept, was the free-standing mahogany fire screen with tapestries of woodland creatures that she had described in the book, the fire screen that Jo's parents had created and that had been part of Jo's life always. And, there was Jo's fabulous peacock room, with magical murals leading to imagination well beyond the walls of their home. What an honor it was to experience the reality of Jo's world.

Reality, when it is as lovely and magical as Wisteria Cottage, can be easy on the eyes and on the heart. Bob and Jo were the most gracious hosts – even to serving traditional English fish and chips – and later, displaying Jo's exciting, unique collection of kaleidoscopes.

Just as there are many thousands of kaleidoscopes with as many colors and designs as the mind can imagine, literally hundreds of haikus have been written in tribute to the beautiful hummingbird. Over the centuries, as the tiny, brilliantly hued birds have flitted from flower to flower, they have also darted into the hearts of poets everywhere. Hummingbirds have been called precious jewels of nature, with wings of silver and hearts of gold. Because they always just keep on going and going, they have become symbols of strength and encouragement, much as Ingrid has grown into her true nature as a healer, encourager and inspiration during the past few years. Awake at dawn, Ingrid, like the hummingbird, begins her day with the rising sun. A haiku, author unknown, describes how Richard must feel when he wakes in the morning and gazes at Ingrid:

> Mountains and the quiet smile
>
> of my wife
>
> a hummingbird darts between us

"Our property has always been alive with hummingbirds. Until I met my hummingbird muse in Costa Rica, our little year-round visitors were simply beautiful air dancers, flashing in and out of our view," says Ingrid. "Now I know that even the hummingbird in Jo Wall's *Crystal of Enchantment* painting was trying to get my attention."

Perhaps the most telling correlation between Ingrid and the hummingbird is in Irene Kelly's beautiful little book, It's a Hummingbird's Life, where she writes "busy, busy, busy! From morning to night, spring to winter, these tiny birds work nonstop."

When she reflects on the "extreme work" that she and Richard performed together for more than thirty years, Ingrid knows now that she literally emulated the tiny hummers that made their home on the mountain, "work, work, working day and night."

Irene Kelly goes on to note that hummingbirds also "perform amazing aerial stunts with their rotating wings, which beat more than three thousand times every minute."

As aerial stunts go, Ingrid's mid-air medical miracle performed on Elizabeth during the flight to Heathrow Airport in April of 2011 was amazing to say the least. And, when it comes to rotating wings, there have been few times in her life when Ingrid was not moving and doing. In fact, her sense of humor was piqued and her natural instincts heightened in the U.K. when Bob Coulson introduced Ingrid to two of his favorite "smile-getters." The first, a "round of applause," actually involves the person giving the round of applause to physically rotate (or spin) in a circle while clapping hands. Bob's second "smile-getter," which Ingrid now uses regularly, is "Hug O'clock!" "Do you know what time it is?" Ingrid asks innocently, and, as the unsuspecting subject looks at their watch, she approaches with her arms spread wide and ready to hug, answering her own question with the words and gesture: "It's hug o'clock!"

Whether moving boulders on her mountain, working with Richard to clear land, hugging, spinning, dashing through airports to exotic destinations, or dancing with joyful abandon wherever music is played, Ingrid's constant motion comes as naturally to her as does the migration of the hummingbirds to Mexico in winter.

A woman who exudes glitter, sparkle and color, spreading joy and loving energy to everyone she meets, Ingrid is absolutely as captivating as a hummingbird. As her tiny counterpart darts from flower to flower seeking sweet nectar, Ingrid dives happily into every adventure life offers, and with each new taste of friendship and fun, she gains strength and encouragement for the ongoing journey.

While blowing bubbles toward the loading dock of the ferry from the Isle of Wight to the mainland in April 2011, for instance, Ingrid enriched the day immeasurably. Attracting many waves and smiles, often accompanied by shouts of laughter and delight from passengers in the automobiles boarding the ferry, she blew bubbles with joy.

"I haven't seen bubbles in years! Thank you!" shouted

a lady, laughing and waving as Ingrid rushed to blow even more bubbles her way. It is that pure, childlike joy that she shares with others – a rare sparkling jewel in today's often gray and dismal world.

At Heathrow Airport, as in every airport along the way during her trip in 2011, Ingrid greeted fellow travelers with a smile and a friendly wish that they enjoy a wonderful journey through life. Often, people will pause and appear puzzled for a moment when they hear her lilting voice wishing them well. Then, invariably, they'll smile back at her, realizing that here is a happy woman who is passing that happiness along to them.

What a wonderful gift!

And, for those few who are unwilling or unable to accept the gift of happiness at face value, Ingrid has spent a lifetime developing the power to embrace rejection with love and meet the negative with a positive attitude. Just as Jesus kicked the dust off and walked on, so Ingrid shrugs off the hurts and travels forward to seek the sweet nectar of happiness that awaits her.

Each time Ingrid forgives and forgets, her healing ability is strengthened and her aura glows more brightly.

"When you've worn a hard hat in a danger zone for more than three decades, you learn to keep on doing what is necessary no matter what," declares Ingrid. "For this hummingbird, there are more beautiful, succulent flowers than weeds out there, and I've discovered that even the weeds have some beauty in them. I intend to keep spreading the joy of the journey with everyone I meet for the rest of my life. It's my destiny to help make the world a better place, one person at a time. Carpe Diem! Seize the day!"

New bride Pat Sager and Ingrid

Ingrid and Stefanee climb

Stefanee

Wisteria Cottage

Pat & GB's Wedding

Enchanted Manor

The Enchanted Manor

Bob
Coulson as
GREEN MAN
Ingrid and
porpoise friend
Isle of Wight
Painted Shoes by
Josephine Wall
Enchanted Manor
Circle of Love
Ingrid &
Stefanee
Wisteria Cottage
Ingrid & Josephine Wall

Favorite keepsakes at Wisteria Cottage

Josephine Wall in front of her beautiful gallery

Ingrid with Jean Hanner, author of "Wisdom of Your Face"

Ingrid and Psychic Lisa Williams

Ingrid and Psychic Sylvia Browne

Ingrid with Louise L. Hay, of Hay House, Inc.

Ingrid and Jenn Coscia of The Animal Rescue and Adoption Agency (TARAA)

Ingrid with Jennifer Kirk of Kirks Folly

Addendum

Ingrid's Intuitive Insights …

What would love do?

If you love someone, tell them.

The hummingbirds remind me that life is rich, colorful and exciting.

I wore a hard hat to protect me from danger. I wore a pink hard hat because I'm proud to be a strong, working woman.

Bubbles float freely through time and space, carrying beautiful messages of hope, love and joy!

The sounds of music and laughter are precious to my ear.

When people ask what nationality I am, I say *upright, biped, human being, planet earth, milky-way galaxy*.

I believe that each person on this earth is equal. All jobs are equal and needed – from the toilet bowl cleaner to the President of the United States – everyone should be treated with love, compassion, respect, honesty – no one is better than anyone else.

One earth … All family.

In our business, we treat all our employees as family.

We all do what we have to do – sweep the grounds, clean the toilets, take out the trash, along with our main jobs as welders, etc.

Always stay happy, healthy, wealthy & wise – full of love, and positive energy.

Have gratitude for everything each day.

Follow your passion.

My husband Richard, the inventor, always told the children as they were growing up, "If it's not yours, if it's not a toy, don't mess with it. Leave it alone."

I don't believe anything I hear, and only half of what I see.

For instance:

People tell stories and it's mostly one-sided – you're not hearing the full story because you're not hearing both sides.

In my younger years, I'd go out with my son, Wayne, and people that saw us would think I was out with a guy who was not my husband. It was my *son*.

I love those three little monkeys – hear no evil, speak no evil, see no evil. I love those little guys! They're great!

Trick me once, shame on you.
Trick me twice, shame on me.

The truth sometimes hurts, but it is the truth.

I raised our children to be of good character, have love, compassion, respect, honesty, help others as much as possible, and treat everyone equal.

I always believed in a Supreme being. Mother God, Father God and Jesus is our brother – these are my personal beliefs, but I respect others' beliefs also.

No one should judge another – only the person themselves can judge their own soul.

In our line of work, the first thing is safety – always be safe, then do a quality job. Make yourself proud.

In life, number one – family, number two – finances – number three – material things.

In work, blame no one. Just do a quality job, help your fellow worker and work together.

Laughter is a good medicine, and it helps digest your food. I once heard a medical doctor say that it really helped digest your food, so I always tell the kids to laugh – it would be a better world if everybody would laugh more.

A smile does not cost anything and a lot of people thank you for it. I get thanked for my smiles all the time!

I was blessed with a big smile accompanied by dimples – to make other people happy. It's always been there, so it's meant to be.

When you're in the womb, the first organ that forms is the heart – the second the brain – so go with the heart first and then send it to the brain – it will be a better world that way.

In work, we refuse to do anything unethical for any company – honesty and quality work is the best policy.

A good honest day's work … do it for a good honest day's pay.

I always told the children this: "Can't never did!"

I learned this from Doc Garland Granger's mother, Isabel: *When you're talking you should be teaching, and when you're listening you should be learning.*

I feel that all religions should co-exist, have respect for the beliefs of others, take what you want out of it and leave the rest.

Prejudice: The inclination to take a stand (as in a conflict) usually without just grounds or sufficient information.

Your mind is like a computer – fill it with knowledge.

I love truth and knowledge.

You learn something every day. Never stop learning.

Be yourself. Wherever you go, there you are.

Have no doubts.

Follow your gut feelings.

There are no coincidences.

In Heaven, I believe everyone is thirty.

There are teachers along life's journeys.

Be grateful for the laughter and even the tears. Be grateful every single day.

I have the hardest time asking people for help. It's very difficult for me. I do it myself, but I'm trying to get out of that and let more people help me when they want to.

The attitude of gratitude is a magnet for true love in all forms.

I help others with their minds, bodies and souls.

My life is like a kaleidoscope full of ever-changing events and beauty, color, knowledge, learning each day.

> It's like a beautiful translucent, bubble – a gorgeous Circle of Love!

Hummingbirds & Hard Hats are such strong symbols for my life – the hummingbirds, a miracle of life, so delicate and beautiful, yet robust enough to survive hurricanes and typhoons in the tropics, and the pink hard hat, symbolic of the extreme work which has been so much a part of forming the woman I am today. A fabulous serendipitous journey … and the best is yet to come! Join me, please!

About the Author...

SUSAN D. BRANDENBURG

Award winning biographer Susan D. Brandenburg (www.susanthescribe.vpweb.com) lives in Ponte Vedra Beach, Florida, and has the great privilege of writing full-length biographies about fascinating people like Ingrid Reeves. A seasoned journalist, genealogist, speaker and researcher, she has written weekly columns and feature articles for local newspapers, as well as articles for local, state and national magazines. As president of Susan the Scribe, Inc., Susan is a pioneer in the field of writing and publishing. Author of seven biographies, she now takes your story from concept to completion. Susan's words are a gift from God. She thanks Him daily for allowing her to preserve the amazing legacies of His children.

Photo by Ingrid Reeves, January 2011

Ingrid Reeves & Stetson Kennedy
Beluthahatchee … July 21, 2011

When I was a child, my dad would come off his ship and meet us in Jacksonville. We stayed in a cheap little trailer park (the only place that would tolerate my mixed-race mother) and I explored the nearby woods and streams, feeling a deep connection to the land. Beluthahatchee brought back that child in me. I felt one with the land again and one with humanity. In this place of peace and harmony, where the spirit of Stetson Kennedy now abides, great things will be accomplished for Fellow Man and Mother Earth.

In January of 2011, I met Stetson in the hospital. I held his cold hand, knew his heart rate was halting, and prayed with every healing fiber in me that this incredible man would have time to do what was needed to perpetuate his legacy forever. On July 21, 2011, he accomplished that goal, presiding over a dynamic meeting of the diverse, vibrant and dedicated board of the Stetson Kennedy Foundation. I was there. I stood with Stetson on his beautiful cedar deck overlooking sparkling Lake Beluthahatchee, and knew in my heart that Stetson's life work would go on. It was on that day that I pledged to donate a portion of the sales of my book, Hummingbirds & Hard Hats, The Ingrid Reeves Circle of Love Story, to benefit the Stetson Kennedy Foundation. Stetson and I are forever bound by our common belief in one earth – all family.

Love, Ingrid Yvette Reeves – August 2011

Gifts from God

As Christians the world over celebrated on the eve of Christ's birth, December 24, 2010, young Joshua Frase joined his Lord Jesus in person. Born to Alison and Paul Frase of Ponte Vedra Beach, Florida in February of 1995 with a rare neuromuscular disease called Myotubular Myopathy (MTM), Joshua was not expected to live past the age of two, but he defied the odds and lived a full and productive life despite his severe physical disabilities. Joshua's funeral on January 3, 2011 at Christ the Redeemer Church on Roscoe Road was attended by hundreds of mourners, including faculty and classmates from Ponte Vedra High School, where he carried a cumulative 4.3 GPA. A youth whose gifts from God included a positive attitude, a great sense of humor and the ability to apply his healthy brain to academics, goal-setting and independent thinking, Joshua's goal was to attend Wake Forest University and become a research scientist specializing in muscle gene therapy in hopes of finding a cure for his disease. Ultimately, through the legacy he left behind, his goal will be realized. The Joshua Frase Foundation (www.joshuafrase.org) was founded by his parents in 1996 with the goal of funding research into a cure for his disease as well as supporting the families of other children stricken with congenital myopathies. Currently, the Foundation funds promising genetic research for stem cell and gene therapy at Children's Hospital Boston, and cell regeneration at Wake Forest Institute for Regenerative Medicine in North Carolina. In the meantime, at the celebration of his grandson's home-going, Joshua's grandfather, the Rev. James Frase, quoted a text-message sent to a friend on Christmas day 2010 by Joshua's 9-year old sister, Isabella: "This is the best Christmas ever for Joshie, but not for us, because we can't see Jesus." Joshua Miles Frase, 2/2/95 – 12/24/2010, was a devout young Christian who closed his eyes on earth and opened them in heaven. He is now fulfilling his favorite Bible verse from Isaiah 40:31: "But they that wait upon the Lord shall renew their strength; they shall mount up with wings as eagles; they shall run and not be weary; and they shall walk, and not faint."

Hummingbirds & Hard Hats, The Ingrid Reeves Circle of Love Story, is truly a book of love and healing. Ingrid Reeves has pledged a donation of One Dollar from every book sold to the Joshua Frase Foundation. The book sells for $20 and can be purchased on Amazon.com or through the publisher's website: susanthescribe.vpweb.com. For information, call 904-962-5131 or 951-926-4407.

CPSIA information can be obtained at www.ICGtesting.com
Printed in the USA
BVOW070108130313

315391BV00001B/33/P